*Dedicated to the victims
of the Green River killer
and their families.*

*A portion of the proceeds from this book will benefit YWCA programs
for homeless and troubled girls and women in King County, Washington.*

Copyright© 2003 by the King County Journal
All rights reserved

ISBN 0-9747038-0-X
First edition
Published December 2003
Printed in Seattle
Published by the King County Journal

Cover photo: Elaine Thompson
Cover design and photo direction: Marcus R. Donner
Book design and layout: Christina M. Okeson

KING COUNTY
Journal

1705 132nd Ave. N.E.
Bellevue, WA 98005
www.kingcountyjournal.com

Gary Ridgway: The Green River Killer

The story of America's most prolific serial murderer,
told by the reporters who covered the case
from the beginning

By the staff of the King County Journal

About the Authors

All of the reporters, photographers and editors who contributed to this book are current or former staff of the King County Journal. All principal authors continue to cover the case for the newspaper:

Reporter Mike Archbold covered and directed coverage of years of searches, press conferences, investigations and funerals before reporting on the 2001 arrest of Gary Ridgway and writing a magazine-length profile of the killer. (Chapters 1, 2, 3, 4, 7, 11, 12, 14, Epilogue)

Reporter Noel Brady has covered court and crime news for the King County Journal for the past five years. He participated in coverage of Ridgway's arrest and conviction. (Chapter 6)

Reporter Nora Doyle normally covers education but switched to crime to report on the biggest plea bargain in the history of American law. (Chapters 13, 21)

Kathleen Merrill was the legal reporter on the Ridgway case and covered its developments including the filing of charges, arraignments, monthly status conferences and his plea deal. She also wrote stories about the victims and their families. (Chapters 5, 19, 20, 21, 22, Epilogue)

Reporter Dean Radford has covered the Ridgway story from the beginning. In 1982 he was working the night shift when the first victim was found in the Green River, and he was sitting in court 21 years later when the killer was finally convicted. (Chapters 8, 9, 10, 14, 17, 20, 21, Epilogue, Timeline, Victims List)

Reporter Bruce Rommel has also covered the Ridgway story from the beginning, and spent countless hours reporting from dump sites, interviewing family members and checking out tips. (Chapter 15)

Reporter Jamie Swift wrote the lead, front-page story covering the Nov. 30, 2001, arrest of Ridgway and has followed the case ever since. (Chapters 16, 18)

Edited by Mike Ullmann and Tom Wolfe.
Additional editing by Caroline Young Ullmann and Jean Parietti.

Table of Contents

Map 8
Introduction 11
Photos 83

Chapter 1: The Boy 15
Chapter 2: The Man 21
Chapter 3: Divorce, Descent 27
Chapter 4: Hunting 31
Chapter 5: Killing 37
Chapter 6: Deception 45
Chapter 7: The Victims 49
Chapter 8: Getting Caught 55
Chapter 9: Dave Reichert 59
Chapter 10: The Task Force 63
Chapter 11: The Polygraph 67
Chapter 12: The FBI 71
Chapter 13: Impatience 77
Chapter 14: A Suspect Again 103
Chapter 15: The Manhunt 109
Chapter 16: The Missing Decade 115
Chapter 17: The Break 121
Chapter 18: The Arrest 127
Chapter 19: The Case 131
Chapter 20: The Deal 143
Chapter 21: Guilty 153
Chapter 22: The Mind of a Killer 165

Epilogue 181

Timeline 185
The Victims 203
Index 206
Acknowledgements 210

Path of the Green River killer

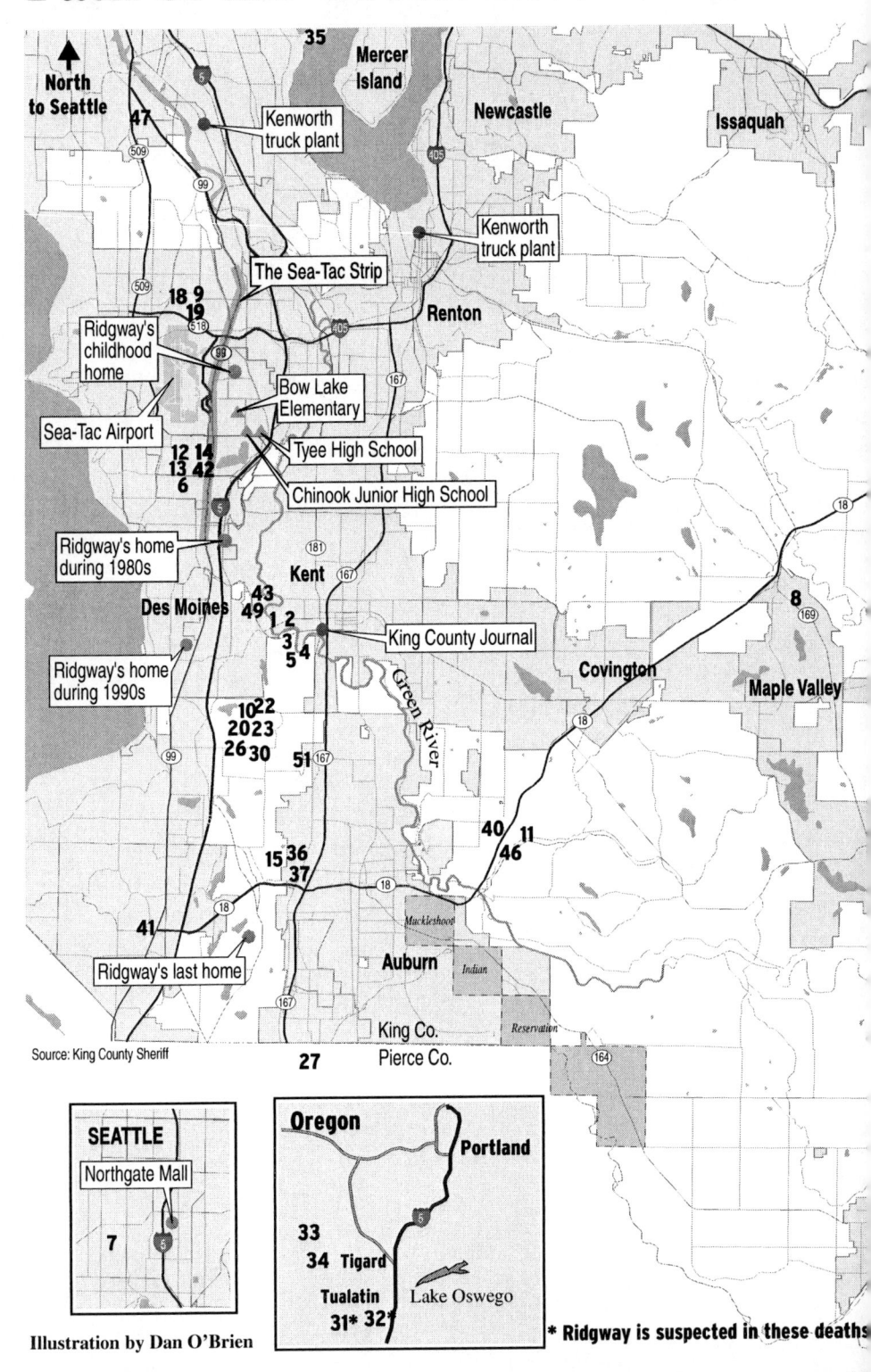

Illustration by Dan O'Brien
Source: King County Sheriff

* Ridgway is suspected in these deaths

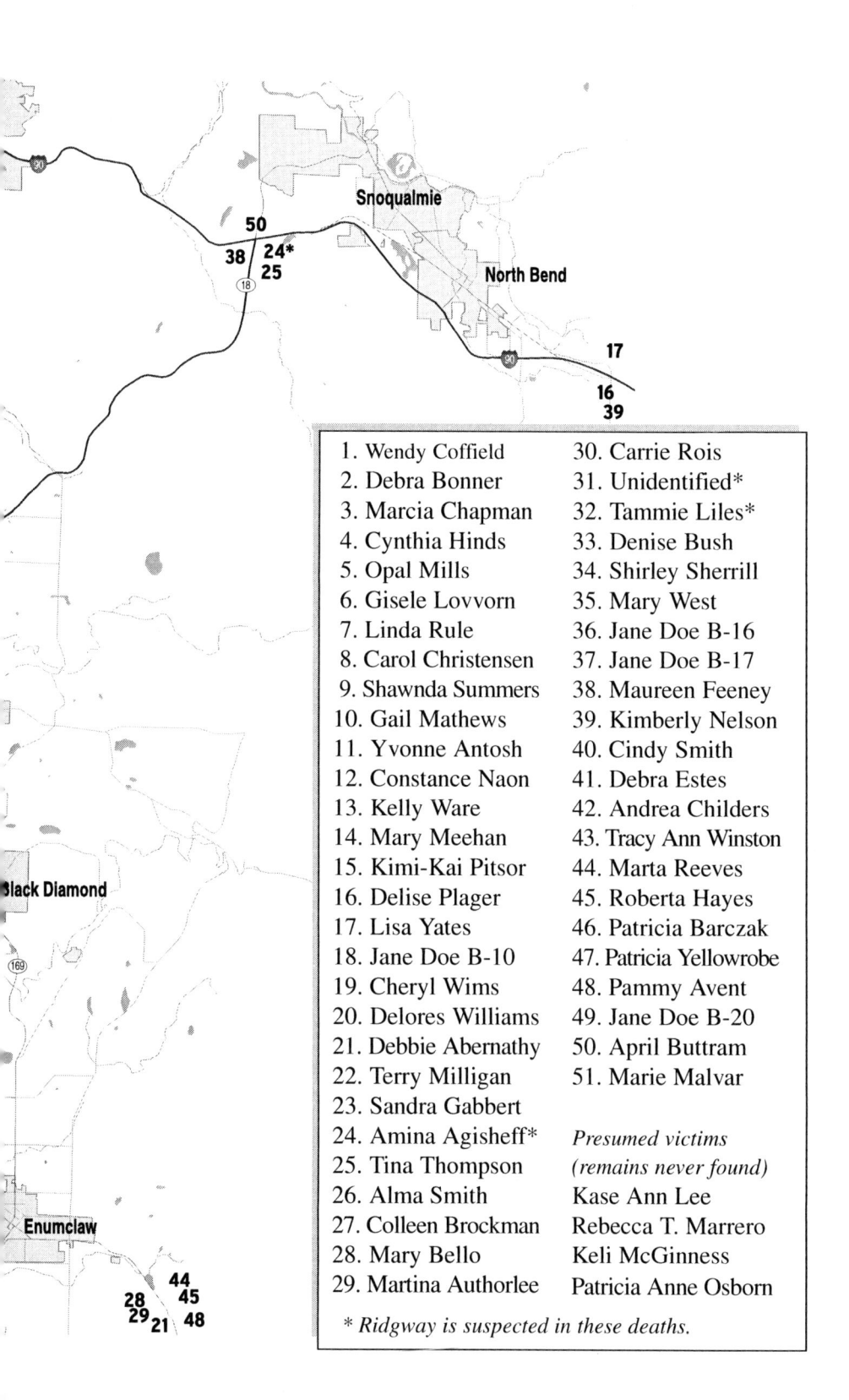

1. Wendy Coffield
2. Debra Bonner
3. Marcia Chapman
4. Cynthia Hinds
5. Opal Mills
6. Gisele Lovvorn
7. Linda Rule
8. Carol Christensen
9. Shawnda Summers
10. Gail Mathews
11. Yvonne Antosh
12. Constance Naon
13. Kelly Ware
14. Mary Meehan
15. Kimi-Kai Pitsor
16. Delise Plager
17. Lisa Yates
18. Jane Doe B-10
19. Cheryl Wims
20. Delores Williams
21. Debbie Abernathy
22. Terry Milligan
23. Sandra Gabbert
24. Amina Agisheff*
25. Tina Thompson
26. Alma Smith
27. Colleen Brockman
28. Mary Bello
29. Martina Authorlee
30. Carrie Rois
31. Unidentified*
32. Tammie Liles*
33. Denise Bush
34. Shirley Sherrill
35. Mary West
36. Jane Doe B-16
37. Jane Doe B-17
38. Maureen Feeney
39. Kimberly Nelson
40. Cindy Smith
41. Debra Estes
42. Andrea Childers
43. Tracy Ann Winston
44. Marta Reeves
45. Roberta Hayes
46. Patricia Barczak
47. Patricia Yellowrobe
48. Pammy Avent
49. Jane Doe B-20
50. April Buttram
51. Marie Malvar

Presumed victims (remains never found)
Kase Ann Lee
Rebecca T. Marrero
Keli McGinness
Patricia Anne Osborn

* *Ridgway is suspected in these deaths.*

The Green River in Kent, where it all started.

Gary Kissel

Introduction

WHEN THE GREEN RIVER is running high, it looks like the khaki-colored water is going to slip over the bank and run right through the front door of the King County Journal office in Kent, in suburban Seattle. That's how close we are to the river.

In summer, the river level falls a good 10 feet and drops out of sight. From across the street, you can't see water, just blackberry bushes, overgrown weeds and a few scrub trees. To see anything in the flat of the river bottom at mid-summer, you have to walk right up and take a good look — or just stumble upon it.

That's what happened July 15, 1982, as two curious boys rode their bicycles along a bend in the Green River, not far from our office. Galen Hirschi, 15, spotted what looked like white tennis shoes snagged on a wooden piling. He thought it was a mannequin. He and his friend, Robert Anderson, waded into the shallow water and instead found the nearly nude body of Wendy Coffield, dead at the age of 16.

The body "was all covered with moss," Hirschi said. "Then I noticed there was a blue Levi jacket pulled over a head, and I saw some hair."

News photographer Duane Hamamura was on duty that day at the Daily News Journal, precursor to the King County Journal. His office then was where it still is today, exactly 1 1/2 miles upriver from that bend in the Green. Hamamura rushed to the scene and took the only photographs of what turned out to be the first recovery of a victim of the Green River killer, photos later published around the world.

Four days later, the victim was identified and detectives knocked on the door of Virginia Coffield in Enumclaw. The agonizing scene would be replayed dozens of times in the years ahead, investigators bringing parents the worst news of their lives. They didn't have to say anything, Coffield told the Journal. "Moms know."

Hamamura recently reflected on the incomprehension of those early days. "I had no idea what was to come," he said. No one did. No one knew this was the beginning of the largest serial murder case in American history, nor that it would take more than two decades to solve the case.

In August, four more bodies were found, all in the Green River or on the bank nearby. Throughout the summer of 1982 and for the next 20 months, teenage girls and women were killed at a voracious pace, triggering the arrests of several innocent men and the largest manhunt ever in Washington state.

Many, perhaps most, of the women were killed during those initial months. But their bodies would be found for years, sometimes one by one, sometimes in "clusters," perplexing investigators.

Twenty-five detectives were mobilized early on, and began to find links to prostitution and street life on the Sea-Tac Strip. At its height, the Green River Task Force staff numbered 56. Techniques its members developed would rewrite the book on dealing with bodies at outdoor crime scenes.

But despite thousands of leads, police couldn't solve the case, and the Task Force shrank. By the early 1990s, one lone detective sat behind a Task Force desk.

Police had questioned the killer — even searched his house — but were unable to develop hard evidence until improvements in DNA science led to his arrest in 2001.

Over the years, dozens of Journal staff members have worked on the Green River story, including several who covered the case from the beginning, in 1982, and are still with the newspaper. Together, Journal staff have taken hundreds of photos, conducted countless interviews, spent innumerable hours at crime scenes, archived cabinets of documents and written more than 1,000 stories, many of them exclusive.

This book draws on that experience, Ridgway's confession as transcribed in legal documents, and an exhaustive court file to tell, for the first time, the entire story of one of the most depraved, prolific serial killers in American history and of the 20-year investigation that finally brought him to justice.

— Tom Wolfe,
Editor, King County Journal

As a Tyee High School senior, 1969

The Boy
Chapter 1

BEFORE INTERSTATE 5 WAS BUILT, Pacific Highway South was the major route between Seattle and Tacoma. Washington Highway 99, its official designation, had always been a rough gathering place of roadhouses, gambling parlors and cathouses. Then, when the Seattle-Tacoma Airport opened in 1947 and went international two years later, more people came. Motels, hotels and diners sprang up, and the commercial district spread, drawing even more people to what became known as the Sea-Tac Strip. The 1970s brought drugs and decay, and by the early 1980s, police had another name for the Strip. They called it the Night of the Living Dead, a procession of streetwalkers, drug dealers, johns and runaways.

This is where Gary Leon Ridgway grew up, and where he always returned.

Ridgway was born Feb. 18, 1949, in Salt Lake City, the middle son of Thomas and Mary Ridgway. His brother Greg was a year older; his brother Thomas Edward two years younger. In 1960, when Ridgway was 11, the family moved to Washington state. His parents bought a three-bedroom rambler in McMicken Heights, a neighborhood that stops abruptly to the west at the Seattle-Tacoma International Airport, central landmark of the Strip.

Clinging to a ridge called Highline, the neighborhood drops sharply to the east into the Green River Valley, where on summer nights residents could see the lights from Longacres racetrack until it closed in 1993.

Longtime residents say the neighborhood hasn't changed much over the years. The houses are small, the lots large. There are few sidewalks. Homes have been remodeled and expanded, but they still have the clapboard look of the 1950s. Pacific Highway South, or Pac Highway, as it is known to locals, slices north and south now as it did then, collecting the hotels, parking lots, restaurants, bars and mini-malls that serve the airport's transient populations. Maps still call it Pacific Highway South, but civic boosters have changed the signs. In 1990, soon after the city of SeaTac was formed, Pac Highway was renamed International Boulevard inside the city, part of an effort to clean up the Strip and leave behind the taint that accompanied the old name.

The Ridgway family home sits back from the street, obscured by a mini-forest of large trees and shrubs. A Monkey Puzzle tree greets visitors. The house remained in the family for 41 years, and Ridgway never strayed far from home, except for a two-year stint in the Navy. Ridgway's father spent time on the Strip, too. Thomas Ridgway was a Metro Transit bus driver, and the Strip was his regular route. Thomas Ridgway died in 1998, but Mary Ridgway lived in the home until Aug. 15, 2001, when she died at the age of 73. After their mother's death, the brothers put the house up for sale, and it sold shortly before Ridgway was arrested in November 2001 and charged as the Green River killer.

•••

Growing up in the 1950s and 1960s, Ridgway earned a reputation for being congenial but not too bright, as he haltingly progressed from Bow Lake Elementary School to Chinook Junior High to Tyee

High School. Classmates and neighbors remember an average kid. Unremarkable, they say: polite, quiet, quick to smile. As a student, he was below average, a slow learner and a poor reader. He earned mostly Ds at Tyee and didn't graduate until he was 20 because he was held back twice. He was athletic, though. Ridgway played football in the ninth grade, and in the 10th grade he got an A in boys' P.E.

Nancy Rudy, who taught more than 30 years at Tyee, barely remembers him: "There was nothing particularly remarkable. He was only on some class committees, and I can't even name those. He simply wasn't involved in activities, so teachers didn't get to know him."

Classmates and neighbors remember a little more. At the time of his arrest, Jeanne (Jewell) Casanova remembered going on a double date 30 years previously with Ridgway. They went to the Midway Drive-In, a fixture on Pac Highway for decades. Today, the drive-in holds a swap meet that Ridgway frequented in recent years, but in those days it drew a younger crowd. Casanova has forgotten the movie but distinctly recalled Ridgway as a lousy kisser. She never went out with him again, but they remained part of the same crowd.

Casanova and her sister, Terry Rochelle of SeaTac, and some of their friends, one of whom lived next door to the Ridgways, helped organize "Teen Nightclub" gatherings at McMicken Heights Community Center in the mid- to late-1960s. The Ridgway brothers would attend, and the two sisters remember them well. Gary Ridgway was a typical teenager who seemed to tag after his older brother, Rochelle recalled. Though he tried to act tough like the older kids he hung around with, Casanova said, "He didn't strike me as somebody who had a lot of anger." He smoked cigarettes. He had acne. He occasionally told off-color jokes, and he was sometimes rude.

"It's shocking and kind of scary," said Valerie Stuart, another Tyee classmate, who remembers seeing Ridgway and his wife at the school's 20th reunion. "I never ever imagined that (he would become a killer). ... He was just kind of there like the rest of us. There were a few standouts, but he wasn't one of them."

Ridgway melted into the life of his neighborhood like most young people. But there was another Gary Ridgway that no one knew about. That Gary Ridgway would come to light decades later.

Bob Pedrin, who now lives in Ridgefield in southwest Washington, played football with Ridgway and graduated with him. But he remembered little else. "There was nothing that would draw your attention to Gary as being different from anybody else," Pedrin said. "He was just a normal guy who was quick to smile. He was just one of the kids trying to make it through school." Later in life Pedrin developed another connection to the Ridgway case. As a former Fire District 43 firefighter in South King County and a member of an underwater rescue team, he was called to the Green River on Aug. 15, 1982, when the bodies of three of the first Green River victims — Opal Mills, Cynthia Hinds and Marcia Chapman — were discovered. He had no idea he knew their killer.

• • •

Glimpses inside the Ridgway home are rare. Patsy Smith, who lived a half-dozen houses up the street from the Ridgway house for 40 years, said she didn't know the family at all. She said the parents did not mingle with neighbors or invite people into their home. When Ridgway's ex-wives spoke with detectives about the Ridgway home and family dynamic, they recalled experiences that were mostly negative, especially concerning Ridgway's mother.

Ridgway's first wife, Claudia Kraig, said that after they were married Ridgway at first kept his mother's name on his checking account and always checked with his mother before making any major purchase. The domineering attitude Ridgway's mother had toward him was one of the points of disagreement in their marriage, Kraig said.

Marcia Winslow, who was married to Ridgway from 1973 to 1981, told King County detectives that Ridgway's mother dominated and was "continually yelling at his father." Once when she and Ridgway visited his parents' home, his mother got so angry at his father she broke a dinner plate over her husband's head while he was sitting at the dinner table. Ridgway's father didn't retaliate; he simply got up from the table and left. Even so, Winslow said, Ridgway was "very close" to his mother and not close to his father.

Stranger was the way Ridgway's mother dressed. She wore tight clothes and excessive makeup, Winslow said. She looked like a prostitute.

Decades later Ridgway told detectives he had a sexual attraction to his mother, that his feelings toward her included lust and humiliation, and that he sometimes wanted to stab her.

•••

Few people saw a dark side to the young Ridgway, but it was there, hidden behind his casual smile and passive demeanor. When he finally confessed decades later, Ridgway told investigators about the first time he spilled human blood. Ridgway was a teenager, 15 or 16 years old, and his victim was a first-grader, just 6. Investigators were able to track down the victim, now 44 and living in California, and get his side of the story. He remembered every detail.

Jimmy Davis was playing near a wooded area close to his home. He was wearing a cowboy hat, cowboy boots, two "six-guns" and a toy rifle. Ridgway approached and asked Jimmy if he wanted to build a fort. The youngster readily agreed. Then Ridgway said: "You know, there's uh, there's people around here that, that like to kill little boys like you." He led the boy into woods where he stabbed him with a knife, passing it through the ribs and into the liver.

The boy told detectives he asked Ridgway "why he killed me. ... I watched too many cowboy movies, you know, and I saw all the blood pumpin' out of me, I mean it was already running down my leg into my boots. The whole front of my shirt was soaked. And he, uh, started laughin', and he had a smile on his face, and he stood there for a minute, and he has his knife in his hand, and he reached towards me and he just wiped the knife off — both sides of the blade, once across my shoulder and twice across my shoulder on the other side. He says, 'I always wanted to know what it felt like to kill somebody.' "

Jimmy Davis spent the next several weeks in a hospital recuperating from the knife wound. The incision to repair his liver was a foot long. He never returned to his school; he was tutored at home for several months and then moved with his family to California. No arrest was ever made.

Ridgway later told investigators he was unaffected by the experience and took no responsibility. "He was in the wrong place at the wrong time, and I was in the right place at the right time, I guess what you'd call it."

At the time, police were unable to verify the assailant's identity. Davis' cousin, Debbie Roberts, regrets that Ridgway wasn't dealt with at the time, nearly 40 years ago. "He might have gotten help that could've prevented all these murders."

Booking photo, 1982

The Man
Chapter 2

FOR MOST OF HIS ADULT LIFE, Gary Ridgway was a married man with a steady job.

The job was at Kenworth Truck Co., where he started before graduating from high school, and stayed for more than three decades except for a two-year stint in the Navy. At work, he received awards for perfect attendance. After his military service, he never lived far from his parents or the neighborhood where he grew up. Most details of his life are utterly conventional, and he looked the part. He was a family man and a homeowner. He had a son. He walked the dog. He drove a pickup, worked on cars, sold Amway products, chatted with neighbors, visited his mother, hung out with co-workers, attended swap meets, read the Bible, went to church, and for a while proselytized door to door, encouraging neighbors to bring God more fully into their lives.

Ridgway was married for more than 20 years, but not to the same woman. And that's where the image of stability starts to break down. His easygoing relationships at work contrast sharply with turbulent relationships in his private life, especially in the gaps between his three marriages.

∙ ∙ ∙

After 32 years at Kenworth, Gary Ridgway was sixth in seniority in the paint department and made about $22 an hour. He usually brought his lunch to work, but sometimes joined co-workers for lunch at Bergie's on Airport Way. He often hung out with a group of about six painters after work.

Linda Blaney, who started at Kenworth in 1978 and was a union leader for years, described Ridgway as gregarious and gentle. She worked with him comfortably even after 1987, when Ridgway was questioned as a suspect in the Green River killings and word spread around the plant.

"I remember he talked to me years ago about being an Amway salesperson. I thought, well, he's not the Green River killer, because he's an Amway salesperson. You would have wanted to go anywhere with him, because he was so harmless. He's not a very big guy," Blaney said. "He looked very well-together."

Ridgway is 5-foot-10 with a slim build and brown hair parted on the left. He weighed 150 when he was arrested in the Green River killings. His choir-boy smile and thick glasses gave him an ordinary appearance. He was meek and nonthreatening, exactly the way he wanted to look. He dressed in jeans, sweatshirts, T-shirts, depending on the weather. As he told investigators later: "My appearance was different from what I really was."

One woman who worked in the paint department with Ridgway for 20 years and considered Ridgway a friend described his painting style as patient and precise. "Some instructors can yell at you, but he was more, 'You need to do it this way,' " she said.

Despite the exacting, tedious nature of their job, she said the painters had fun together: "I think Gary enjoyed his job," she said. "The thing that bugs me the most is that everyone pictures him as this psychotic loner. That's not the guy I know."

Ridgway sometimes shared pictures of his son, Matthew, and talked about his garage sales. During his single years, he talked about getting dates from the personal ads in the Little Nickel and picking up prostitutes, which offended some co-workers.

•••

Ridgway met Claudia Kraig the summer he graduated from high school. They were married a year later, on Aug. 15, 1970, at the Fort Lawton Chapel in Seattle by a military chaplain. He was 21; she was 20. In a 1986 interview with detectives she described him as normal sexually, and very social.

Shortly after marrying, the young couple moved to San Diego, where he was stationed in the Navy. He then shipped out for a six-month tour in the Western Pacific, leaving his wife at home alone.

Navy medical records indicate Ridgway had a venereal disease in December 1970. Years later he mentioned to a girlfriend that he disliked Filipino prostitutes due to his experience during port calls in the Philippines while on his sea tour. Military records also noted that Ridgway was diagnosed with gonorrhea in December 1969.

The marriage was short-lived. When Ridgway returned from his tour in the Western Pacific, Kraig admitted she had had an affair with a mutual friend. Ridgway returned to his McMicken Heights home alone and was discharged from the Navy in July 1971.

The couple tried to reconcile. Kraig returned to live with Ridgway but it didn't last long. They divorced on Jan. 14, 1972.

Ridgway later said his wife had become a "whore" while he was overseas.

•••

Ridgway's second wife describes a man who was much less social and much more preoccupied with sex.

Marcia Winslow met Ridgway in late 1972 on the Renton Loop, a cruising route in downtown Renton. They hit it off immediately and lived together for a year before marrying Dec. 14, 1973. They rode bicycles on Frager Road along the Green River in Kent past the Meeker Street Bridge, often stopping to pick blackberries and have sex in the tall grass by the river.

The couple lived in various places in Renton, Federal Way and West Seattle. She said her husband spent most weekends at his parents' home. Their son, Matthew, was born Sept. 5, 1975.

She told detectives that Ridgway viewed her as a sex object and housekeeper, asking for anal sex and on a couple of occasions tying her up. He would often ask her to perform oral sex on him while they were driving around. He preferred sex outdoors, she said, including a variety of places in King County, some of which later became dump sites for his victims: along the Green River in Kent and Highway 18 toward the Cascade foothills, on State Route 410 in Greenwater east of Enumclaw, and the North Bend area along Interstate 90. Unlike the social person described by Ridgway's first wife, Ridgway had no outside friends during their marriage, Winslow said.

He also developed disturbing habits. Winslow told detectives that one night when she and Ridgway were returning from a party, he grabbed her from behind and choked her using his hands until she was able to break free. Ridgway admitted the attack to detectives in a 1986 interview. He practiced walking noiselessly, and he was good at it. He also used to sneak around corners and scare her, placing her in chokeholds. He carried clear plastic tarps and a blanket in both their car and truck. He told her that the garage was his private place and to stay away from it.

With the birth of their son, Ridgway became "fanatical" about religion. The family attended a couple of churches, one Baptist and the other Pentecostal, and proselytized door to door. At night, Ridgway would sit in front of the TV with an open Bible in his lap. He would frequently cry during or after church services. His religious fervor ended when they separated in 1980.

In 1981, they divorced. There was such animosity and mistrust that each filed a restraining order against the other. In an interview with detectives prior to his guilty plea, Ridgway opined that some of the blame for the murders should be placed on Winslow. If he had killed her like he wanted to when they divorced, it might have "changed my life. I'd only have one (murder) instead of 50 plus."

Matthew left with his mother. Ridgway had Matthew on alternate weekends and was ordered to pay child support of $275 per month. But he was mostly on his own. Soon the killings would start.

Perhaps they had already started. After his arrest, Ridgway told detectives that it was "very possible" that he killed a woman in the 1970s while living in Maple Valley with Winslow. He described one incident, claiming he could not recall any details except that "some'n went wrong, uh, with the date and I, I killed her."

Count 48 of the statement of charges against Ridgway referred to Jane Doe B-20, whose unidentified remains were found along the Kent-Des Moines Road. Investigators said she died sometime between July 6, 1976, and Aug. 31, 1993.

Ridgway led investigators there, saying he murdered that woman in 1982, 1983 or perhaps in the 1970s.

Ridgway's memory of the women he killed was poor, but he knew where bodies were buried.

Patrick Hagerty
The home where Ridgway killed most of his victims.

Divorce, Descent
Chapter 3

ON CHRISTMAS EVE 1981, Gary Ridgway walked into a Parents Without Partners social at the White Shutters Inn on Pacific Highway South. It was the first Christmas since his divorce from Marcia Winslow, and he was visibly shaken. He sat down with Sharon Hebert, whom he had met recently and begun dating, and started talking.

He had nearly killed a woman. He said it several times. From the way he described picking her up, Hebert assumed she was a prostitute. Ridgway's clothes weren't ruffled, he had no visible wounds, and he never said exactly what happened, but he was clearly upset.

Several years later, Hebert described the incident to detectives. Hebert doesn't seem to have inquired about the details of a near murder, nor let the incident get in the way of their relationship. Contrary to accounts from other girlfriends, Hebert described Ridgway as gentle, caring and sexually "well mannered." They had sex at least twice a day, she said, adding that she thought he could engage in sex six or seven times a day.

Hebert continued to see Ridgway until May or June of 1982, when Roxanne Theno, another woman from Parents Without Partners, told Hebert that Ridgway was frequenting prostitutes and had given her herpes. Only then did Hebert end their relationship. It would take the threat of the death penalty before Ridgway would ever again talk about killing.

•••

In the months and years after his separation and his May 27, 1981, divorce from Marcia Winslow, Ridgway juggled a string of relationships, one of them resulting in marriage. He was considered a prodigious lover by girlfriends who said he often demanded sex two or three times a day.

Throughout these relationships, Ridgway also frequented prostitutes, a practice he said began in the Navy. Even before he started killing, there were hints of violence in those encounters.

Ridgway's first adult contact with police occurred in 1980. A prostitute accused Ridgway of choking her while they parked on a dark street south of the airport. She ran to a nearby house and called Port of Seattle police, who handle the airport. Port police contacted Ridgway, who said he had retaliated after the woman bit him while giving him oral sex. They let him go. On May 11, 1982, he was arrested for soliciting a police decoy on the Strip; he would later take precautions against being trapped again. Ridgway continued to have steady girlfriends.

In May 1981, he met Nancy Palmer through Parents Without Partners. She told Green River detectives that her first sexual encounter with Ridgway occurred outdoors, in a bunker at Fort Casey on Whidbey Island in Puget Sound. He moved into her West Seattle home, and they began having sex as many as three times a day, anywhere and everywhere.

On two occasions he tied her up for sex, one time outdoors to wooden stakes driven into the ground. The idea for bondage came from a pornographic movie they both watched. Marcia Winslow had told detectives she had gone through a similar sexual experience, but Ridgway went further with Palmer, sometimes inserting grapes and bananas into her vagina.

Otherwise, Ridgway was withdrawn. Their lack of a social life beyond sex contributed to the end of their relationship, Palmer said. In December 1981 she asked him to leave, and he did.

In January 1982, Ridgway moved into a small, three-bedroom house he had purchased in November 1981 at 21859 32nd Place S., in the SeaTac area off Military Road South. In that house, over the next two years, Ridgway would kill most of his victims.

He did his best to give the place a nonthreatening appearance. He set up one of the bedrooms for his alternate weekends with his son, Matthew, who turned 7 that year and whose toys and clothes gave the home a look of casual, disheveled normality.

Theno, the woman who told Hebert that Ridgway had given her herpes, met Ridgway about this time. She usually saw him on weekends, and usually at Theno's house. It was easier that way, because of her two children.

Theno and Ridgway continued to attend Parents Without Partners dances for the next year and a half while dating, seldom going to any other social events. Theno told detectives that she saw women at Ridgway's place on two separate occasions and realized he was not a faithful boyfriend.

She continued to see Ridgway anyway.

Theno and Ridgway were to be married in June 1984, but she called it off. She said Ridgway didn't seem to mind. In early 1985, he met Judith Lorraine Lynch, who moved in with him several months later.

Bob Haven knew Ridgway from January 1982 to 1989, as a next-door neighbor in the small SeaTac neighborhood. He said his memories of all those years are not detailed, but he did remember that Ridgway married his third wife, Judith Lynch, in the Havens' front yard in 1988.

Haven's wife was listed as a witness on the Ridgways' marriage certificate.

The wedding was a neighborhood event. Neighbors brought over their lawn chairs.

"He was a likable guy," Haven said, echoing the feelings of neighbors at two of Ridgway's other South King County homes. "They didn't socialize much." He knew they liked to go camping and Haven viewed Ridgway as an outdoor person.

Even after Ridgway's arrest in 2001, Haven supported Ridgway. "I've got a good feeling he is innocent," Haven said, although he added, "I could be wrong."

The Sea-Tac Strip in the 1980s.

Hunting
Chapter 4

GARY RIDGWAY TOOK PRIDE in his skill at hunting victims, at picking the right girls from the streets, the ones who would be easy to kill. His initial technique was simple: Drive through areas of prostitution and keep his eyes open. He called it "patrolling." He would spend hours before and after work, patrolling.

He picked prostitutes because they were available, vulnerable and hard to trace. "Uh, prostitutes were the easiest," he told investigators. "I went from having sex with them to just plain killing 'em."

He knew where to look. One good spot was Pac Highway between his house off Military Road South at South 218th Street, and South 188th Street near the south end of Seattle-Tacoma International Airport. Ridgway estimated he picked up and killed at least 15 prostitutes along that stretch of the highway.

The Riverton area in Tukwila along Pac Highway was really good hunting, he later told investigators. He found most of his victims there. He also patrolled along Pac Highway south from Des Moines to Federal Way, in South Seattle's Rainier Valley, through the International District in downtown Seattle and downtown Seattle itself, and up to Aurora Avenue in North Seattle. Aurora Avenue was the name of Pac Highway north from downtown Seattle.

Spotting a target, he'd make eye contact or flash money as he drove by, then pull off the road into a parking lot. He would wait for the woman to approach alone. He rarely picked up a woman at the curb. He was afraid of witnesses — other prostitutes, pimps, waitresses, passers-by — who might link him to a murder. When not actually driving, Ridgway would patrol by parking in areas where he might not be noticed. A favorite ploy was to pull into a convenience store along Pac Highway, pop open the hood of his truck as if he were having car trouble, and then check out the action. Hotel parking lots were good cover, too.

His victim's race wasn't of great concern. "I'd much rather have white," he told detectives. "But black was fine. It's just, just garbage, something to screw and kill her and dump her."

He was more particular about age. He liked his victims young, in their teens, new to the streets. Most of his victims were under 20. They were relatively innocent and less likely, he said, to "con" him. Ridgway noted that "the young ones" tended to plead more earnestly for their lives. "I talked to them before I had sex with them and she'd say, 'I've only done this a few times before.' ... I mean if she's 13 or 14 years old ... you figure that's true. If you get one that's 20 and 25 that talks the slang and everything and they say 'I've only done this a few times,' they probably got an arrest record and they're lying. But the young ones stood out more when they talked when they were dying."

Ridgway said that during his most active period, he slept only a couple of hours a night and devoted the rest of his free time to hunting, killing and the disposing of bodies. "There were a few women that for some reason I didn't kill, but they were few and far between."

He hated it when he invested time finding a victim, then couldn't lure her into his truck. "I'm really mad at some of 'em because I ... didn't get a chance to pick 'em up," he told detectives. "They want too much ... the pimp was following me or somethin' ... I just lost one, the next one I'm gonna do everything I can to sweet talk her. I'm gonna kill this one and I'm gonna strangle her head ... strangle her neck so it ... it breaks."

With his middle-age, middle-class look, prostitutes sometimes mistook him for an undercover cop. He started carrying beer in his truck and offering it so the women would "know I wasn't a cop, relax with me." At least 50 women asked him if he was the Green River killer. His reply: "Do I look like the Green River killer?"

Ridgway believed that police would not look hard for missing prostitutes. They were constantly moving from place to place, city to city. Missing persons reports were rarely filed on them, and if one was filed, police had trouble finding out when the woman was last seen. He also knew police and prostitutes were not on friendly terms.

He had other ruses to put women at ease and get them to trust him. He'd say he'd be a regular customer. He'd offer to lend them a vehicle, to get them jobs, to feed them. He never worried about keeping the promises, because, as he told detectives, "they were already dead." He invested in the future by giving rides to women with companions. He knew he couldn't pick them off and kill them then, so he'd act helpful. Next time he saw them they might be alone.

He even used his young son to gain the confidence of victims. "So every time I opened my wallet there would be a picture of my son on one side, uh, you know, behind my ID. ... And they'd see that and lower any big defenses." He put kids' toys on the dashboard of the truck when he went hunting for victims. A dad with a little boy isn't going to hurt anyone.

Ridgway needed privacy to kill the way he liked, by strangulation. So if a prostitute was afraid to go to a remote location or his home for their "date," he would simply go ahead with the "car date," hoping that the next time she would feel more at ease. An extra benefit: if he was ever caught, those women could serve as references, telling police he didn't hurt them. They would be like an alibi: Sure he dated prostitutes, but he didn't kill them. There was also the spare-tire-in-the-front-seat trick. He'd place the tire there, then complain there was no room for sex in the front seat. Why not go somewhere and get out of the truck? He normally paid $20-$30, but would offer more money if a prostitute would accompany him to a wooded area or his house. How could he lose? He'd get his money back, plus any extra cash of hers.

Hunting required that he stay in the right mood: calm and easygoing. Missing a chance to kill infuriated him, and he had to calm down to continue the hunt. "I couldn't all of a sudden pick up another woman and still be in that frustration," he told detectives. "I'd be in the mood right then to get her in the car and choke her. But with the ... I had to calm down to get ... so I wouldn't look like I was, you know, scared and shaking." If a victim noticed something wrong, he had an excuse. "Well sometimes like I ... I'd be anxious because of the frustration with the first one and I'd be shaking but I'd have to bring it on the side that I just got arrested a couple of weeks ago for prostitution and you can see I'm a little bit nervous."

He looked for undercover cops working the Strip. He would watch women from a distance to see whether they picked up tricks, and he often waited to pay for sex until after the woman got into his truck. He asked prostitutes to show him their breasts or vagina before he would agree to pay. Ridgway believed undercover officers would refuse to do that.

After he was transferred in the late 1990s from the Seattle Kenworth plant to Renton, Ridgway told prosecutors he continued to hunt for victims. The crack epidemic had arrived and Ridgway found that sex with cocaine-addicted prostitutes was cheaper than ever. In early interviews after his arrest, Ridgway denied killing during this period, but later said he was "semi-retired." The truth was that Ridgway continued patrolling for prostitutes — and may have continued to kill — until the day he was arrested. In his confession, Ridgway once admitted killing relatively close to the time of his arrest in November 2001, but denied remembering any details. Nor could he say for sure the last time he killed.

He made a few mistakes. On May 11, 1982, just before his killing spree began, he was arrested on Pac Highway after agreeing to pay for sex with an undercover King County police officer. Almost two decades later, just before his arrest in November 2001, he was arrested for the same offense, again with an undercover decoy. His hunting technique hadn't changed. He waved money from the window of his parked car, then drove out onto the highway and parked in a motel parking lot. The decoy officer walked over, but Ridgway told her he had seen a police officer watching and suggested they meet in a bank parking lot down the street. She agreed, and Ridgway was arrested.

Once he picked up a prostitute intending to kill her, but mistakenly took her to a scene where he previously had left a body. His "date" became upset at the sight and insisted they leave. Ridgway gave her a ride away from the area, returned and buried the body. The police were never told of the incident. Another time his urge to kill led him to try to kill two women in one night. It was a definite mistake, he said, because a witness at that spot had seen the first woman get into his truck. On the night of March 3, 1983, Ridgway killed Alma Smith, dumped her body and was back on patrol within an hour. When he was turned down, he finally called it a night.

But he still didn't get caught. He continued hunting. He was good at it.

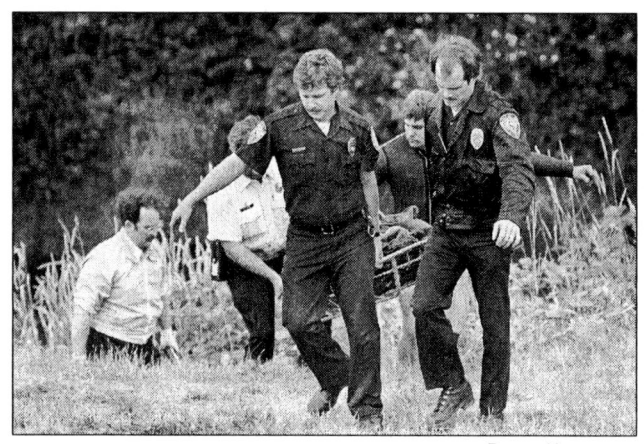

Kent Police officers Randy Bourne, left, and Rob Kellams, right, help carry the body of Wendy Coffield from the Green River.

Duane Hamamura

Killing
Chapter 5

PRACTICE MAKES PERFECT, whether the craft is cooking, building or killing. Gary Ridgway practiced his craft, his "career" he called it — searching for vulnerable young women, earning their trust, having sex and killing them, then discarding them like trash — over and over for two decades.

He thought about killing night and day. He knew how to get the job done without making a mess, without making a scene, without making anyone — including the victims themselves — suspicious. When the women did catch on, often while his arm was wrapped around their necks and they realized this "date" had taken a disastrous turn, it was too late for them to do anything but beg for their lives. And often they would do so: "Don't kill me;" "I'm too young to die;" "I've got family I'm taking care of;" "I've got a daughter at home;"

"I don't want to die." Those frightened pleas didn't do any good. None of those women got away.

Ridgway studied killing, learning from trial and error. What was the best method to snuff out a life? How could it be done quickly and quietly? How could he do it again and again and not get caught?

As he practiced his craft, he got inordinately good at it. Although a poor reader with a limited education, he was successful time and again, throwing police off his trail with ruses and planted evidence. "For a man who barely graduated from high school, Ridgway had what appears to be an innate understanding of forensic evidence," detectives would admit.

He practiced until killing became, by his own description, quick and simple. He had strangling down to an art that took just minutes. He would later brag he could pick someone up, have sex, kill and dispose of the victim within an hour.

And he admitted to doing it at least 60 times, maybe 70, without mistakes, although there were certainly missteps along the way. Over what might turn out to be as much as a 30-year killing spree, nothing would trip him up — not the "date" he accidentally took to a site where he had dumped a body, not the times people saw him with women who later turned up dead, not the one who got away.

Once he got women into the bedroom of his SeaTac home — or his truck, whether it was his own or one he borrowed from family members — they were doomed. Most of the victims were killed in his bedroom, he later told police, although one did nearly make it out of the death house alive. She reached the front door, but he caught her and killed her there, just inches from safety.

• • •

Women are vulnerable when they're naked. That was a key factor at the beginning of the end for many women and girls — his getting them as naked as possible. To achieve that goal, he would negotiate for them to give him "half and half," oral sex followed by intercourse. He would offer them more than they would usually make, to sweeten the deal. After all, he wasn't going to pay. He would take the money back before they were even cold.

Taking women home was best, to an environment he could control entirely. No interruptions, no surprises and he knew the terrain better than anyone.

He encouraged them to go to the bathroom before they had sex, knowing from experience that his strangled victims became incontinent upon their death. "I don't, I was in the idea of getting them in there and killing them. I didn't want them to shit in the bed. So that was the main reason," he told police in his confession.

If the women he killed did urinate or defecate as they died, he would throw his bedding into the wash, then go and dump the body, then come back, put the bedding in the dryer and wait for it to finish.

Ridgway developed a technique that began with positioning the woman naked, on her hands and knees, facing away from him, with her neck thrust out and exposed. To guarantee that position, he would tell his victim that he could only have an orgasm if he entered her from behind. He would wait for the victim to raise her head, then he would, literally, move in for the kill. "And after I got behind them, penis/vagina, I would climax and usually the woman would raise her head because, you know, the guy's through, I can get dressed. Usually when she raised her head up, I would wrap my arm around her or put something around her neck and choke her," he said.

If they were in the back of his truck, covered by a camper shell, he would "warn" them of an approaching vehicle. "I'd tell 'em 'here's a car coming,' so guess what, she lifts up her head like that ... She's not thinking anything of it. Her hands are down normal and it's my time to wrap my arm around her neck and to choke her and not have ... get in the way of her mouth. I got bit in the hand with a mouth one time ... But it's my idea to get her head up so I could get a clear shot of her neck to kill her."

Of course, the women struggled. But he learned ways to deal with that. One technique was particularly effective: I'll let you go if you stop struggling. When they stopped struggling, they were easier to kill. "But I wasn't gonna let her go. It was just my way of lying to her to keep her from fighting. She stopped fighting and I just kept on chokin'."

He never shot or stabbed someone, he would later tell police, because "it would have been messy" and his victims might still be able to scream, a deadly consequence for him in his tightly packed neighborhood where some houses are mere feet apart. There was an even darker reason for strangling his victims: "'Cause that was more personal and more rewarding than to shoot her." Personal was compressing someone's neck in the crook of an arm and using the other arm to add leverage.

Still, many women struggled mightily before they lost consciousness and he would wrap his legs around them for a double hold. If his right arm got tired, and they weren't struggling too much, he would switch arms. Sometimes, he would roll over onto his back, squeezing with his arms and legs. Sometimes, he would roll the victims onto their backs and stand on their throats.

He learned some women had more fight in them than others. He was scratched, and one such incident left him with deep grooves in his left arm; he poured battery acid on them to disguise them. He still has the scars. He sometimes resorted to using ligatures instead of his bare arms, including towels, a belt, a bathrobe tie, extension cord, rope, necktie, socks, jumper cables, a "tieback" for a curtain, and his T-shirt.

He never experimented with different ways to kill his victims. "I didn't because my method's working pretty good. Choking is what I did, and I was pretty good at it."

•••

Ridgway told police he didn't torture or cause his victims unnecessary pain. But he continued to molest them once life had left them. He set fire to one woman's hair, but put it out when he got worried that someone would see the smoke. He tried, by pumping on her chest, to bring one woman back to life after killing her in the back of his truck.

But the thing that turned the stomachs of people interviewing him during the months of confession to 48 slayings was that he had sex with the bodies of victims. A few were so decomposed that maggots had appeared.

"That would be a ... uh, that would be a good day, an evening or after I got off work and go have sex with her. And that'd last for one or two days till couldn't ... till the flies came. And I'd bury 'em and cover 'em up. Um, then I'd look for another ... Sometimes I killed one, one day and I killed one the next day. There wouldn't be no reason to go back."

His motive? "Just wanted sex. And it was free. I didn't have to pay for it. I killed her."

Risky behavior wouldn't deter his need to have sex with some of the victims again. He returned to the body of one victim, and had sex with her, while his young son lay sleeping in his nearby truck. But it was more difficult for him to climax with corpses, and he eventually stopped doing so, he said, because it became less satisfying. "Something fresh instead of someone who is cold."

The admission of necrophilia seemed to solve another mystery investigators had puzzled over. They found some victims they had thought had been deliberately posed: on their backs, their legs spread in unnatural positions. But Ridgway's explanation for this was simple. Once rigor mortis had set in, he "often had to forcibly spread their legs apart" to have sex with them. Then he simply left them the way they were, he said.

Ridgway sometimes brought his obsessions to work.

He killed one woman before his shift, then drove to Kenworth with her body in the back of his truck. At lunch, he drove to the murder site and had sex with her body. Then he returned to work, her body still lying in the truck.

He also took the jewelry of victims and left it in women's bathrooms at work. There, his co-workers would find watches, earrings, rings. That they would wear the jewelry of the women he killed thrilled him. "And my favorite thing was maybe if someone's walking around with a piece of that jewelry that they found in the bathroom."

•••

"I have a burden of having to find a place to put it."

That's how Ridgway described having to dispose of his victims, a chore he resented. It wasted his time and money, driving around looking for a place to put them, and kept him from killing even more women.

"Then if I could uh, take 'em and drop 'em in the bottomless mine shaft, uh, uh, every, every one of 'em, and I could'a had uh, then I would have a uh, much clearer mind at, at, at killing more women, not spending the time finding locations was the, was a big burden. Took the time away from killin'."

In most cases, he would dump the body quickly, usually within half an hour after the slaying. To get a body out of the house undetected, he devised a system as methodical as the killings themselves. He would drag the body off the bed and wrap it in a sheet of plastic or a rug, drag it through the house, back his truck up to the door, open the tailgate and slide the body inside. To give himself some cover, he would unscrew the light bulb by his kitchen door. Once he snuck a body out of his house inside his young son's footlocker.

He dumped most of them naked or nearly so; less evidence that way. He disposed of their clothing because "they were just rags to me."

Dumping the bodies was easy.

"He would drive, usually at night, to a secluded spot, park his truck, and quickly pull the body out of the vehicle and dump it just off the roadway," prosecutors detailed in court documents. "Then, he would drive up the road and park just far enough from the body so that if the vehicle was approached by a police officer, the body would not be discovered. Then, making sure no motorists could see him, he would walk back through the woods to the body, and drag it farther from the road."

He did worry his victims might regain consciousness during the trip, and he tied ligatures around the necks of some of them before putting them in the truck. He'd watch his rearview mirror for any movement as he drove to his chosen location.

He placed bodies by "landmarks" — large trees, guardrails, hills, large fallen logs — something he could locate again later. Putting bodies in clusters made it easier for him to know if they had been discovered, so he could avoid those sites later on. "Clusters so I won't forget where they ... where they are ... So, I've done it before and, ah, just easy. When ... if I drive by and think somebody's been ... you know, found 'em then that way I would stay away from them."

Some victims were buried in shallow graves, to keep the smell of decomposing remains from leading to their discovery. He covered many victims with brush, branches and other debris — "she's garbage, so I put, ah, stuff over her that was garbage."

Most victims were left off roads in heavily wooded, remote areas, some of them so steep that police had to use ropes to lower themselves to sites in their searches for remains.

Ridgway did receive minor injuries during the killings and dumpings. He'd report some of those at work: "If I got hurt like pulling her because of her weight and it bothered me I'd just blame it on work so State Industrial would pay for it," he told police.

* * *

During Ridgway's rampage of killing in 1982-84, the only victims found soon after their deaths were Carol Christensen and those in his first cluster along the Green River. In the coming years, police would find remains at other dump sites so badly damaged by time and nature that little or no evidence was forthcoming. But in those first victims, police found the DNA evidence that would ultimately be the killer's undoing.

Ridgway was angered when those bodies were found, he said after his arrest. "It felt like they were takin' som'n, some'n a' mine that I put there." He also learned important lessons from those discoveries: Don't return to the same place too many times. Leave bodies in remote areas.

It would be the beginning of many lessons he would learn that would keep police from touching him for nearly 20 years. And applying those lessons, he continued to practice killing.

Mark Morris
Detectives Fae Brooks, Rick Gies and Dave Reichert search for evidence at the site north of Sea-Tac Airport where the remains of Shawnda Leea Summers were found in August 1983.

Deception
Chapter 6

THE PROFILERS WERE WRONG.

The Green River killer wasn't an outdoorsman or a loner. He didn't have uncontrollable bouts of anger or a known criminal past. He appeared to be a dedicated father, a reliable employee, basically a nice guy. "My appearance was different from what I really was," Gary Ridgway would eventually tell detectives.

Ridgway's double life — easy-going company man at Kenworth Truck Co., murderer of at least 48 young women — defied expectations. "Those who thought they knew Ridgway best did not know him at all," including his wife and brothers, King County prosecutors wrote in court documents. "Ridgway deliberately cultivated the innocuous aspects of his personality. ... In this way, he conned scores of victims who had survived years using street-smarts."

As a teenager, Ridgway was a slow learner. There's no evidence that he ever studied forensics. Still, Ridgway knew what he was doing. At the wooded areas where he dumped their bodies, he left nothing that would identify him. When a struggling victim scratched him, he clipped her fingernails so that no particles of his skin would be found. And when detectives twice searched the bedroom where he confessed to killing most of his victims, they found not a trace.

"I was in a way a little bit proud of not being caught doing (anything) like removing their clothes, not leaving anything, any fingerprints on it, using gloves, not bragging about it, not talking about it," Ridgway said.

If he met a victim through her pimp, he would call the pimp after killing her and ask to see her again, to suggest he had no knowledge she was dead. If there was a witness when he picked up a prostitute, he sometimes went through with the date, both to cultivate prospective victims by establishing a street reputation as a "good date" and to establish support for his story to police that he simply enjoyed the services of prostitutes. He planted cigarettes and gum used by someone else near bodies, hoping to lay a false trail. Once he left a hair pick, thinking police would suspect a pimp. He scattered leaflets from airport motels in a ravine where he'd left the body of Marie Malvar, hoping that if police ever found the corpse they'd suspect the killer was a business traveler. He then planted her driver's license at Sea-Tac Airport to raise the possibility she had left town.

Ridgway was on the Green River Task Force list of possible suspects, knew as much, and cooperated willingly during encounters with police through the mid-1980s. He routinely admitted to dating prostitutes and even said he was addicted to them. His candid answers made him more believable. In 1984, Ridgway even agreed to take a lie-detector test, repeatedly denying any role in the Green River murders. The examiner concluded Ridgway was telling the truth.

Unlike most serial killers, police never found any incriminating "trophies" from Ridgway's victims when they searched his homes. In most cases, Ridgway stripped his victims of their clothes and jewelry and disposed of them separately.

In 1983, he left a most atypical victim in a wooded part of Maple Valley. Unlike most of the dead women, she was clothed. She was lying on her back. Two trout were placed on her chest, an empty wine bottle across her stomach and sausage on her hands. That provoked all sorts of speculation about religion, ritualism and sacrifice. But it may have been just a red herring. Ridgway later confessed that he posed the body, using items he happened to have in his house when he killed her.

In early 1984, when the Task Force expanded and suspicion of Ridgway grew, he sent a mysterious letter to the Seattle Post-Intelligencer. Typed with neither punctuation nor spacing, the letter entitled "whatyou_eedtonoabouthegreenriverman" mentioned evidence privy only to detectives and the killer, such as the fact that some of the victims were raped after death. The note suggested the killer was a traveling salesman or a long-haul truck driver, and might be using a knife or a gun. The letter did its job. It became one more puzzle piece that didn't seem to fit.

That spring Ridgway loaded his truck with camping gear, his 8-year-old son and the bones of Denise Bush and Shirley Sherrill, and drove to Tigard, a suburb of Portland, Ore. To his son, it seemed like a typical camping trip. The real purpose: to hide the remains of the two women far from Ridgway's home and usual hunting grounds. Ridgway used only cash and left no evidence of the journey. After his arrest, he admitted to detectives he tried "to throw you guys off (and) think the bodies were down here in Oregon and killed in Oregon." To some extent it worked. The Task Force focused on the Portland area for several months.

But the biggest thing Ridgway did that allowed him to continue killing, undetected, for nearly 20 years, was to keep his mouth shut. "Ridgway's success at eluding police can be attributed in part to his remarkable ability to remain silent," prosecutors wrote.

"For decades, Ridgway gave no one who knew him — relatives, spouses, girlfriends, co-workers, acquaintances — any hint that he was a murderer. Until his arrest in 2001, it seems, Ridgway told absolutely no one that he had killed."

Gary Kissel
Kathy Mills, on the fifth anniversary of the death of her daughter, Opal, in 1987.

The Victims
Chapter 7

BEFORE THEY BECAME Green River murder victims and before their young lives became defined by prostitution, they were daughters, sisters, girlfriends, wives and mothers.

Twenty-nine of the 44 identified victims of Gary Ridgway were teenagers. The 10 youngest were 15 or 16, children just a few years past playing with dolls and snuggling with a favorite stuffed animal. Some lived with parents or relatives. Some were in foster care. Many were on their own, living on the street. Only a few had established criminal records of prostitution. All were simply trying to survive.

Stories of street kids and runaways today are the same as those heard two decades ago. A family history that involves sexual abuse, drugs or violence is common. So is the feeling of being unwanted. At 15 or 16 years of age, street kids have seen more of life than adults twice their age, but abuse can stunt emotional growth, and they often have the decision-making skills of an 8-year-old.

Street kids often start out as couch surfers, drifting from one place to the next until one day it is time to pay — pay for rent, pay for food, pay for drugs, pay for protection. There is always someone around to tell them how to make a quick buck. Sex always sells. They had "boyfriends" who doubled as pimps, but often they really were just boyfriends about their same age. Together they struggled to survive.

It was dangerous, but teenagers think they are invincible.

Not all of Ridgway's victims were young or relatively new to the streets. A number of them had been on the streets for years, hard-core prostitutes who traveled the West Coast circuit from Los Angeles and San Francisco to Seattle and Vancouver, British Columbia.

To their families, friends and even to themselves, many of the younger Green River victims denied they were prostitutes. Sure, they sometimes traded sex for money, but only to get by. The late 1970s and early 1980s were tough economic times, especially for a young woman without job skills or a high school diploma. And help from social service agencies was more scarce then than it is today.

Prostitution helps explain how these young women became victims, but it doesn't define them. Many of the parents angrily insist that their daughters are better defined as troubled, rebellious, high-spirited teenagers. The only real commonality among the 48 victims was that Gary Ridgway killed them. Each had her own story.

• • •

What angered one Kent teacher about the death of 16-year-old Opal Charmaine Mills was the loss of potential she saw in Opal.

Opal was the fifth Green River victim. Her body was found Aug. 15, 1982, in the Green River cluster in Kent, along with two other Ridgway victims, Marcia Chapman, 31, and Cynthia Jean Hinds, 17. The two teenagers knew each other.

Sandra Cross was Opal's math teacher at Kent Junior High School. "She was just a smart kid; she just let her mouth get her into trouble sometimes," Cross remembered. Opal had a volatile temper that could explode into a stream of obscenities and could cool as quick as it erupted.

With her temper also came a sense of humor. She loved to laugh and tease. More streetwise than her schoolmates, Cross said Opal's joking included bragging that she "hooked on the side." No one believed her; she was just talking.

Opal had fallen behind her classmates in reading and math and was placed in a special education class. Her biggest problem, Cross said, was skipping class. It kept her behind. Her absences finally got her expelled from school that spring.

A school counselor recalled Opal "used to cry about things, but wouldn't explain it."

Her father, Robert Mills, who died in 1991, was angered when police said his daughter and the other victims had ties to prostitution. "I'm pretty damn hot. I talked to that goddamn detective, and I told him I have no reason to believe my little girl was in prostitution," he said after his daughter's body was identified. He said his daughter wasn't a "whore. She was just in the wrong place at the wrong time."

Kathy Mills, who is now a secretary to the senior minister of New Directions Ministry in Kent, wrote about her daughter in a book she published in 2002, "Through a Mother's Eyes." In her book, she revealed how her husband sexually abused Opal and how Opal ran away from home after Robert Mills returned to the home after a yearlong absence.

A week after she left, Opal was dead.

Opal had told family members she was going to meet "Cookie" to do some painting to earn money. Cookie was Cynthia Jean Hinds, who disappeared about the same time as Opal. Their bodies were found together.

Kathy Mills doesn't believe Opal was a prostitute, either. But she acknowledged that Opal liked to hitchhike, stayed away from home for weeks at a time and hung out with a bad crowd who frequented Pac Highway.

She wrote that her daughter's "vision for the future was to have a lot of children and just give her life to looking after them. Opal simply adored kids. She had a friend living near Olympia who had a baby. She would go those 40 miles just to babysit."

At Opal's funeral, the Rev. James Young of the Light House Temple Church warned that young people must be careful. "This is a very rotten society. Let what happened to Opal ... rest on the minds of other girls because what's happened to Opal could happen to them."

Opal also knew Wendy Lee Coffield, 16, whose body was the first one found in the Green River, on July 15, 1982. They had attended Kent Continuation High School, an alternative high school, in 1980 and 1981.

A teacher there remembered that they were friends, but they were also both loners who liked to hitchhike. The teacher had given them a videotape to warn them about the danger of taking rides from strangers.

• • •

Deniece Griffin was 15 years old when her two teenage friends, Opal and Cynthia, disappeared. Now an adult and a military service veteran, Griffin still misses them dearly. "I always call them My Friends in the Sky," she said.

The girls may have been out on Pac Highway, but she doesn't think they were involved in prostitution. Perhaps they were simply hitchhiking, she said. Griffin explained that parents had told them that only bad girls hung out along the Strip, which gave Pac Highway an attractive sense of taboo.

"It was a challenge to see who could get out there first," she said. The idea "wasn't to be a prostitute but to just go to a notorious place to say you had been there."

Griffin remembers Hinds as a 17-year-old, coming to their home at the Rainier Vista housing project to babysit her little sister. "She was the type of person who wanted to be happy," she recalled. "She loved life. She always stood up and looked out for the younger children."

Deniece said Opal and Cynthia were her last female friends. After losing them, she found it difficult to establish a similar bond.

• • •

Virginia Coffield said in an interview in 2001 that she saw God's hand at work in those horrible events nearly 22 years ago when her daughter, Wendy, was found in the Green River.

"God probably took her for a reason," she said. "He didn't want to see her on the streets and into drugs. ... What can you say about your daughter. I love her. I can feel her around me all the time."

Born in the spring of 1966, Wendy lived most of her life in South

King County or farther south in the Puyallup area in Pierce County. There wasn't always much money in the family. For a time, they lived in a tent in the foothills of the Cascades, picking and selling blackberries to pay for necessities. Her mother and her father, Herbert, divorced in 1979.

School was hard for Wendy, and she didn't like it. She preferred to play baseball. Her mother said Wendy couldn't "comprehend things well."

Mother and daughter moved into a low-income housing project called Springwood Apartments southeast of Kent. Wendy was caught stealing clothes from the complex's laundry room. With a cousin, she began getting tattoos.

As she moved into her teen years, Wendy rebelled. At 12, she and a friend had run away to a truck stop looking for a ride to anywhere. Later, she was arrested in Eastern Washington in a stolen truck with other teenagers and was eventually placed on probation in King County. She stole lunch tickets at Sumner Junior High School and in May 1982 took food stamps from a neighbor.

Her mother had a boyfriend, and she admitted that her daughter slept with him once. All three of them struggled with alcohol problems. Another arrest for forging checks led to a court-ordered evaluation that found Wendy needed the support of a group home. Her mother agreed.

Wendy was placed in the state's temporary custody. She was put in a temporary receiving home near Tacoma. On July 8, 1982, she got approval to visit her grandfather but was told to be back the next night by 9 p.m.

She never returned. Her short, rough life ended in the Green River.

••

One teenager who did not seem at the time to fit the mold of the other Green River victims was Maureen Sue Feeney, 19. Her remains were found in May 1986, a few miles from her Issaquah home.

She had never been on a list of missing women considered by the Task Force to be possible victims of the Green River killer. Task force officials made her the 35th victim because of her age, sex and the fact her remains were found within 1 1/2 miles of two other victims.

At the time she was found, her parents released a statement saying that their daughter was the exact opposite of previous victims who were juvenile runaways and associated with prostitution.

Born in Bellevue and raised in a rural setting, she was described as a member of a close-knit family who loved children, animals and nature. She was devoted to her family and helping the underprivileged.

After high school, she attended Bellevue Community College, taking courses in early childhood education. She moved to Seattle's Capitol Hill a month before she disappeared, with plans to get a job teaching underprivileged children. She worked at a day care and visited her parents on weekends.

But something apparently went wrong in Maureen's life.

Her co-workers said later they noticed a change in her attitude and behavior. She met a new boyfriend who later told police that Maureen got involved in prostitution but denied — implausibly, according to prosecutors — knowing any details of her activities.

On Sept. 26, two jaywalking tickets were written to "Kris Ponds," a probable alias for Maureen. Ponds had the same description, birth date, telephone number, address and employer as Maureen. Jaywalking tickets were commonly written to suspected prostitutes.

On Sept. 27, 1983, Maureen quit her job. Her boyfriend reported her missing the next day. Her family spent considerable time trying to find her.

Twenty years later, Ridgway admitted to killing a girl matching Maureen's description. He had picked her up in Seattle and killed her in the back of his truck. He also pointed out where he had left a body. It was where Maureen was found.

Marie Malvar

Getting Caught
Chapter 8

MIDWAY THROUGH his deadliest round of killing, Gary Ridgway got caught.

On April 30, 1983, 18-year-old Marie Malvar was working a bus stop along the Strip. At about 9:30 p.m., Robert Woods, Marie's pimp, watched as Ridgway pulled his dark-colored pickup to the curb and struck a deal. Marie climbed in, and Woods followed because the two looked like they were arguing. Ridgway headed north on Pacific Highway and turned into a motel parking lot. A few minutes later, with Woods still following and Marie still in the truck, Ridgway headed back south, turning east onto South 216th Street. He was just a few blocks from home. It was dark, traffic was heavy, and Woods lost them when he stopped for a red light.

A few moments later, Marie and Ridgway got out of his truck. Marie had agreed to go to his house for their "date." After sex, Marie became terrified when Ridgway twisted her pantyhose around her neck. In her struggle to survive, she deeply scratched Ridgway's inner left arm.

Later that night, Ridgway headed for Mountain View Cemetery in Auburn to dump Marie's body. But he found another site just to the north that he liked as much. It was a steep ravine off 65th Avenue South that wound up the hill between Kent and Auburn.

Marie was gone, but police would soon have a suspect.

The intersection of Pacific Highway South and South 216th Street is the exact spot where, just a few weeks earlier, on April 10, Gail Mathews' boyfriend, Curtis Weaver, saw her for the last time. Like Marie, Gail was in a pickup truck heading east on South 216th. Her body was found Sept. 18, 1983, near Star Lake.

With Mathews, Ridgway ignored his own cautious practice of backing off a kill if he was first seen with the woman. Mathews' boyfriend tried to get Gail's attention, but she was staring ahead, almost trance-like. Years later, Ridgway told police that Gail did not notice her boyfriend, but it appeared the man on the street knew her.

The boyfriend variously described the color of the truck as greenish and blue, with a canopy. Based on his description, the Task Force issued a bulletin for a man described as a white male, late 20s or early 30s, with curly brown or dishwater-blond hair, driving a pickup that could be a late 1960s or early 1970s Ford, blue with circular primer spots and a cab-high canopy. Ridgway didn't own a truck like that, so the description never led to him. They would learn years later that the description did fit a truck owned by Ridgway's brother, who lived nearby. In 2003, Ridgway admitted borrowing the truck from his brother and using it to transport at least one of his victims to Star Lake, after which he repainted the truck.

In Marie's case, her pimp got a good look at the pickup Ridgway was then driving. It was an older model, dark-colored, with primer spots on the wheel well of the passenger side and no canopy, a description that also fit other disappearances. When Marie didn't turn up, Woods went looking for her. Marie's younger sister, Marilyn, remembers him pounding on their door. Marilyn told her father, Jose, that Marie was missing, and the father went looking for the truck. Jose Malvar searched frantically for days and finally spotted it parked at 21859 32nd Place South, the small, one-story home of Gary Ridgway. Woods also found the truck, and both reported their discovery to Des Moines police.

Court documents related to the Green River case tell a slightly different story, and that is one of the Malvar family's many frustrations. When they filed charges against Ridgway nearly 20 years later, prosecutors made no reference to Jose Malvar's search for the truck that spirited off his daughter. Instead, they wrote that Woods found the truck and called police. Jose Malvar can't understand why he wasn't taken more seriously: "I was the one who brought police to Ridgway."

On May 4, four days after Marie disappeared, Des Moines Police Detective Robert Fox knocked on Ridgway's door. It was the first time those investigating the murders confronted Ridgway face to face. Fox explained why he was there, and Ridgway lied. He said he was out of work and had nothing to do with Marie's disappearance.

But he had more to hide. He didn't want the cop to see the scratches on his left arm, so he stood against the fence in his yard. Later, he burned his arm with battery acid to disguise the scratches. The burns were so deep that the scars are still visible.

Fox filed a report, and Ridgway was worried. He went back to the ravine and searched for three hours for Malvar's body. He couldn't find it. But he left behind leaflets from airport motels on the Strip, hoping to implicate a traveling salesman if Malvar's body was ever found. The ravine was almost inaccessible — a perfect place to start another "cluster." But he never returned. He discovered a co-worker lived nearby. And he knew that police could connect him — however tenuously — to Marie Malvar if her body was ever found.

Court records indicate that at that time, police did not pursue an investigation of Ridgway. There was no warrant to search Ridgway's truck, and no one kept an eye on him. Police said there wasn't enough evidence to pursue him.

Ridgway went right on killing.

He killed Carol Christensen the day before Fox knocked on his door. Her body was found in Maple Valley on May 8. By the end of May, three more women would disappear; 1983 was Ridgway's most productive year.

On July 16, 1983, Detective Fox gave an interview to the Kent Daily News Journal (now the King County Journal) that offers some explanation for the failure to pursue Ridgway after being led to him by Marie's pimp and family. There had been unconfirmed reports that Marie had been seen in Seattle, and Fox concluded that she had simply run away: "I think that she doesn't want to call home."

Rumors persisted that Marie had moved to Hawaii or was working in Hollywood, but Fox's thinking was not shared by others. On July 15, 1983, Marie Malvar became the seventh person listed as a possible victim of the Green River killer.

Twenty years later, with the threat of execution hanging over his head, Ridgway finally admitted that he killed Marie. Based on his confession, investigators searched a steep ravine near Auburn, where Ridgway had dumped Marie's body and then failed to find it himself. On Sept. 28, 2003, they found bones. On Sept. 29, they found more, and two days later dental records finally put the matter to rest. Two decades after investigators first knocked on Ridgway's door, Marie Malvar would be returned to her family.

On Oct. 9, 2003, a ceremony was held at Washington Memorial Park in SeaTac, just off the Strip, not far from where Jose Malvar found Ridgway's pickup. A father's wait was finally over. "I know where my daughter is," Jose Malvar said after the funeral.

Jose Malvar now lives in the Philippines, where he has tried to start over.

He has a new daughter. Her name is Marie.

Matt Brashears
Sheriff Dave Reichert talks to the media in March 2002 at Task Force headquarters. At left, Reichert in 1986, his fourth year on the case as a detective.

Dave Reichert

Chapter 9

ON SUNDAY, AUG. 15, 1982, King County Detective Dave Reichert went to church.

Shortly after he and his family returned home, the office called. The bodies of two women had been found in the Green River, not far from PD&J Meats in Kent. They were just upstream from where the body of Wendy Coffield had been discovered July 15 and the body of Debra Bonner found just three days before. Reichert knew the riverbank was brushy and muddy — he had already spent time there — so he changed into jeans.

As other detectives processed the scene where the bodies of Marcia Chapman and Cynthia Hinds were found, weighted down by rocks, Reichert worked the perimeter. Starting at the river, he worked his way up the bank, through blackberries and 6-foot-tall grass, looking for evidence. Assisting him was the keeper of his photo log, Sue

Peters. Their search together for the Green River killer would last another 20 years, as Reichert rose through the ranks and became sheriff. Suddenly, the young Reichert froze, not in fear or confusion but to avoid disturbing evidence. At his feet lay the body of Opal Mills, 16, of Kent.

"I've found another one," Reichert called out. Other officers came running as Reichert and Peters laid out police tape and recorded the scene.

Reichert later returned to the river to help with the recovery. The bodies had been there for some time. As Reichert started to lift, pieces of decomposing flesh slipped through his hands. Reichert went home that night "absolutely exhausted mentally and emotionally." He didn't sleep well, but he knew his own kids were at home safe and alive.

As the investigation began to unfold — and sometimes unravel — Reichert and his family would lose that sense of security. Already a 10-year veteran with the King County Police Department, Reichert had known fear and near death. He was known as a cop's cop. On a domestic violence call, a man once jabbed a knife deep into Reichert's throat. Twice he was recognized for valor, and colleagues knew he would cover their backs. Nearly 20 years later, as sheriff, Reichert would order sharpshooters to take out a man who went on a deadly rampage in Shoreline, north of Seattle. It was, he said, his most difficult decision.

But it was the decade of the 1980s — the decade of the Green River killer — that would define Dave Reichert as a cop and set him up to become sheriff and a possible candidate for governor. Reichert spent a long, frustrating decade trying to solve the Green River case. He fielded calls day and night and responded to most because any one could be the call that would break the case open. As lead detective in the case, Reichert triaged tips and investigated the ones he developed. Many were scribbled on paper; eventually, the Green River Task Force got a computer to help keep track of evidence — and suspects.

In a 1984 interview, Reichert acknowledged the strain of the investigation: "I always have had a positive attitude, but I get down sometimes. I don't like to lose, not even at checkers. ... After you work something two years and don't see an end, the more obsessive you become in trying to solve it, and the pressure hits you." As a father, Reichert could see that his three children were affected, too. "If they get asked where Daddy is, the answer is 'out digging out another body.'"

Those early years weighed heavily on Reichert. So did the images that played in his head, and the unforgettable smell of some of the dump sites. His personality changed. He became aloof, and worse, ignored the family that meant so much to him. There had been missteps and miscommunication early in the investigation, and Reichert felt the sting of criticism. The media and victims' families clamored for an arrest. Then things got personal. Two suspects threatened Reichert and his family with death. For months, his family lived under 24-hour police protection. Officers followed his children to school.

Finally, in 1986, four years after the first victims were found, "I realized my family was growing up, and I was missing it," he said later. Reichert credited his wife, Julie, and their strong Christian faith for sustaining him and their family through those difficult years.

Seven years into the case, Reichert was still determined, but he had become more philosophical: "I'd be lying if I said I never thought of trying something else, because this has been one of the most difficult things I've ever done in my life," he said in a 1989 interview with the television news program "20/20." "Sometimes it's like beating yourself against the wall, but you drive yourself." Asked in a subsequent interview for a prediction of when the case would end, Reichert's response proved remarkably accurate: "I don't know whether it will be the 10 or 12 years I have left, but eventually I think we'll find out who this guy is." Reichert was right. Ridgway was arrested exactly 12 years later, and it was Reichert who made the announcement.

The media spotlight was always focused on Reichert, with his athletic, square-jawed good looks and his easy accessibility. He tried to deflect what meager praise was offered to the Green River Task Force to those detectives working with him. This was a team effort. Tom Jensen was one of the key players. To many, Jensen was the hero for keeping the Green River flame alive in the 1990s and for keeping up with technological advances that would eventually link Gary Ridgway to some of his victims. So were Randy Mullinax and Jim Doyon, who tracked Ridgway from the beginning and were the two detectives who arrested him on Nov. 30, 2001.

Reichert alone couldn't track down thousands of suspects or investigate tens of thousands of tips. But often it was Reichert who knocked on the door to tell parents their daughter was dead, and that she might have become a target after getting involved in prostitution.

The first times were the worst, because he simply didn't know what to say. Then he learned the easiest thing to do was just to say it: "I am Detective Reichert. I work homicide and robbery. We just found your daughter. I am sorry to say, but she is dead." The parents would collapse or beat on his chest. They would talk, and Reichert would listen. Then he would have to start his job, trying to find out who killed their daughter. For two decades, Reichert was motivated by promises to parents that he would stick with the case until he found out who killed their children.

On April 1, 1990, Reichert was promoted from homicide detective to sergeant in charge of the deputies who patrol Pacific Highway South. Little was left of the team that for much of a decade had searched for the Green River killer. Reichert's rise through the ranks would continue until, in 1997, he was appointed to replace James Montgomery as director of the King County Police Department, as it was then called. Montgomery became the new police chief in Bellevue, a wealthy suburb east of Seattle. Later in 1997, Reichert became the first sheriff elected, rather than appointed, in King County in decades. As always, the Green River case remained in his thoughts. In 2001, he asked his top lieutenants to take a fresh look at the evidence. He never gave up.

Reichert had been there the day the Green River case began, and he was determined to be there the day it ended. As a detective, sergeant and then sheriff, Reichert kept in touch with victims' families through the years. That was one thing they had come to depend on — that Reichert would always be there for them. And he was. He served as a pallbearer at one victim's funeral. In the days leading up to Ridgway's guilty plea on Nov. 5, 2003, Reichert met with all the victims' families, one at a time or by conference call, to update them on the case, answer their questions and explain why the county was offering the nation's most prolific serial killer a plea bargain. Reichert was also with them in Judge Richard Jones' courtroom on Nov. 5 when Ridgway pleaded guilty to 48 counts of aggravated first-degree murder.

As Reichert left the courtroom, the families applauded. Their journey together was over.

Officers Mike Hagan and Randy Gehrke gather evidence along the Green River where the bodies of Marcia Chapman, Cynthia Hinds and Opal Mills were found in 1982.

Jim Bates

The Task Force
Chapter 10

IN THE SUMMER OF 1982, those living on Frager Road along the Green River were no longer sleeping well. Over the course of a month, five bodies were found in that section of the river, all of them girls or young women, and it was now clear that a serial killer was at work.

The discovery of three bodies in one day on Aug. 15 mobilized police. Days later, a Task Force of 25 officers was formed to bring the killer — or killers — to justice. It would be two years before the bigger, more official Green River Task Force was formed. But even now, the hunt for the Green River killer was the state's largest such homicide investigation since Ted Bundy, a University of Washington graduate and campaign volunteer for former Gov. Dan Evans, started killing beautiful long-haired women in the early 1970s.

Investigators soon gathered thousands of pieces of evidence and considered hundreds of possible suspects. They found out just how hard it was to track prostitutes who lived an elusive lifestyle and often used fake names. Much of their work in 1984 and later years focused on the disappearances of 27 young women in 1983. In several cases, there were no bodies to match the disappearances, and to this day, the remains of two of those 27 missing women have never been found.

Everyone had a theory about the killer: a drifter, a loner, a hunter, a sadist, a rogue cop. Kent psychic Barbara Kubik Patten had her critics on the Task Force, but she was offering more than theories. All she had to do was follow her visions. On April 20, 1984, with her two children in tow and detectives just a mile away, Patten walked almost directly to remains hidden under a crumpled piece of black plastic. She alerted detectives who were searching about a mile away. Patten had a peculiar feeling about the wooded area near North Bend, where human remains were found just days before in heavy brush close to Highway 18 and Interstate 90. About two years later, the remains she found were identified as those of 22-year-old Tina Thompson. Thompson nearly escaped Ridgway in the early morning hours of July 25, 1983, but he caught her at the front door of his house and killed her there.

Ridgway didn't fit any of the official or popular profiles, nor did a psychic or anyone else on the periphery of the case track him down. But on the street, he had come under suspicion. By early 1984, he was starting to get a little careless, asking too many questions of prostitutes, and at least one was starting to connect the dots.

On Feb. 3, 1984, Dawn White, who worked the Strip as a prostitute, contacted the Task Force about her suspicions that Ridgway was the Green River killer. She described him to police as "weird and different." It was from White — and later Ridgway's own comments — that detectives got the impression that Ridgway didn't like black prostitutes. Ridgway, out hunting for victims, approached White and a fellow prostitute, who was black. Both got into Ridgway's truck. He was nervous about cops and asked for identification to prove they weren't police decoys. White saw his ID, too, as she considered whether he had enough money for both of them. He said he didn't, and he chose White, a white girl, over her black friend.

Sitting in Ridgway's maroon pickup truck outside a market on

South 144th Street, White noticed a roll of plastic in the truck bed. Ridgway wanted White to wait while he ran to buy something for his pickup, maybe wire or a fan belt, something, White considered, that could be used to choke her. Now she was feeling uneasy, but before anything more happened, county police came by and made White and her friend leave the parking lot.

White did more than report Ridgway to police. Based on her glimpse of his ID, she also found Ridgway's number in the phone book and gave him a call, tipping him off about police interest in their interaction. Later, Ridgway agreed to meet with Dawn White and her boyfriend/pimp at Randy's Restaurant on East Marginal Way in Seattle. He described the various venereal diseases he had contracted. The meeting lasted about an hour. Ridgway acted like he had a guilty conscience, White told police.

After her phone call, the killings appeared to stop.

The 49th victim of the Green River killer, believed for years to be final victim, was Cindy Anne Smith, 17, who had disappeared while hitchhiking on Pacific Highway South, on March 13, 1984. More bodies were found after that date — a total of 14 victims of the Green River killer were recovered in 1984, more than any other year — but they were all girls and women already on the list.

The toll was staggering. In less than two years, the Green River killings had become the largest unsolved serial murder case in American history. In the glare of national attention, county officials found the political resolve to commit more resources to investigate the thousands of tips, suspicions and possibilities.

In early 1984, the Green River Task Force was officially formed, and the number of investigators expanded to 36. To get detectives closer to the action, the Task Force was relocated from downtown Seattle to the sheriff's Burien precinct. Their quarters were cramped and spartan. Computer and phone lines dropped from the ceiling. One detective couldn't get up from a chair without the person behind scooting closer to the desk. Worse, there were no windows and no air conditioning — and many of the detectives smoked.

But with the Task Force came a new resolve. "The man hasn't quit (killing). He's not likely to quit. We're, frankly, tired of it," said Capt. Frank Adamson, who commanded the force.

As the investigation kicked up a notch, Detective Randy Mullinax first investigated White's story about the "weird and different"

Ridgway, and then investigated Ridgway himself.

A routine background check revealed that Ridgway had been arrested in a prostitution sting on May 11, 1982. He had been driving his maroon 1975 Dodge pickup with a white canopy. But Mullinax also discovered that another detective, Larry Gross, had interviewed Ridgway on Nov. 16, 1983. That interview was the result of Des Moines detective Robert Fox contacting Ridgway at his home just after Marie Malvar disappeared seven months earlier.

Court documents offered no insight into what Ridgway told Gross, but Ridgway was now permanently on the Task Force's radar screen.

The discoveries of bodies in isolated areas near secondary roads showed them the killer knew the area and local roads. He was able to drive around day or night and he was big enough to carry adult women up and down steep slopes. After analyzing work records and receipts for purchases for such things as gasoline, investigators determined that Ridgway was "available" for 29 of the murders.

Detective Mullinax interviewed Ridgway at the Task Force headquarters on April 12, 1984. The questioning went beyond White's tip. Another prostitute had told police that the last time she saw her friend Kim Nelson, was Nov. 1, 1983. She was getting into a pickup like the one Ridgway drove. There was also a police report that linked Ridgway and his pickup with Keli McGinness. Both Nelson and McGinness were considered Green River victims, although Ridgway denied in his 2003 interviews with police that he killed McGinness. He would change that though and in 2003, he told detectives that he killed her, suggesting multiple sites where he may have left her body. Her remains have not yet been found.

In a taped statement in 1984, Ridgway acknowledged frequenting prostitutes along the Strip. He talked of dating up to 10 women on the Strip and catching a venereal disease at least three times. He was driving his maroon pickup at the time or his father's brown and tan pickup. He told of seeing Kim Nelson on South 144th Street near the Kentucky Fried Chicken restaurant. He revealed his interrupted "date" with Keli McGinness, but he lied about the date it occurred, or he remembered it wrong.

Ridgway had become a suspect, and they weren't through with him yet.

Mark Morris
Detectives Dave Reichert, left, and Randy Mullinax at Task Force headquarters in 1986.

The Polygraph
Chapter 11

Gary Ridgway surfaced again and again during the Green River investigation. He admitted having sex with prostitutes who later disappeared. Detective Randy Mullinax, hoping to settle the question of whether Ridgway was the killer, decided it was time to give him a lie-detector test.

Ridgway had been cooperative in an earlier interview on April 12, 1984, and agreed to cooperate again. On May 7, he came in for the polygraph test without an attorney, which had the effect of diminishing suspicions. A transcript of the test, administered by Norm Matzke of the King County Police Department, hasn't been made public. But prosecutors acknowledge that Ridgway was asked if he killed any of the victims, and that he said no.

Unbelievably, in the most pivotal event of the early investigation,

Ridgway passed. When the results of the test conformed with the results of a follow-up investigation, "Ridgway was considered to be cleared as a possible Green River suspect," according to court documents. In fact, at that time Ridgway had already killed more than 40 women, including one, Cindy Anne Smith, just a few weeks before the test.

Ridgway later expressed pride in deceiving investigators and explained that he was completely unperturbed about taking the test: "I just was, I just relaxed and took the polygraph. I mean, I didn't practice or anything. Just relaxed and answered the questions and whatever came out, came out."

Ridgway's name never appeared publicly at the time. In 1987, when reporters found out the Task Force was searching a house, they learned Ridgway's identity from neighbors. But his name was not used in newspaper accounts of the search, and when nothing came of the search warrants, the Kenworth truck painter disappeared from public view. And continued his killings.

Two independent polygraph experts who later reviewed the test results found that Matzke's examination of Ridgway was incomplete and therefore invalid. But at the time, it was enough to get Ridgway off the hook. There were plenty of other suspects out there.

In fact there were thousands, according to investigators, though there were only a dozen or so on the "A" list — and some of them weren't so lucky, or so deceptive. Most of the suspects — persons of interest, as investigators liked to call them — didn't surface publicly, except in the rush to solve the case early on.

When the body of the first victim, Wendy Coffield, was found in Kent on July 15, 1982, Kent police began the investigation and quickly landed on a possible suspect: Richard Allen Plemons, 23. A Kent resident, he had been charged first with rape, then with attempted murder by strangulation of a 14-year-old Kent girl the month before. The girl was from the West Hill of Kent, close to Pac Highway.

In August 1982, Larry Darnell Matthews, 31, who was on parole for manslaughter, was picked up by Tacoma police. He reportedly knew and had threatened one of the victims, Debra Bonner, 23, of Tacoma. A woman who described herself as Bonner's best friend said Matthews had threatened to kill Bonner over money that her pimp owed him.

That same month an arson suspect, Thomas Blake Armstrong, 29, from the Des Moines area, was being investigated for the stabbing death of a 15-year-old prostitute whose body was found two months earlier near an apartment complex where he lived.

They never graduated to prime suspects.

In October 1982, a prime suspect in the case emerged in a California prison. John Norris Hanks, 35, was linked to five strangulations of young San Francisco women between 1972 and 1978. He also was being considered a suspect in at least eight other murders.

Named a suspect in the six known Green River killer slayings at the time, Hanks refused to take a lie-detector test. King County detectives including Dave Reichert visited Hanks in prison and returned with blood and saliva samples. Hanks later agreed to a lie-detector test and to an interview with detectives. After the test, the Task Force said he was no longer a suspect.

About the same time as Hanks, Melvyn Foster, a cab driver who knew some of the victims, piqued the interest of detectives by volunteering to help on the case. He soon became a prime suspect. Foster also submitted to a lie-detector test, but unlike Ridgway, he failed, even though he was innocent. Based on the results of that test, detectives obtained search warrants to look for evidence at the Olympia-area home where he lived with his father. Foster said detectives took a rock-polishing machine, clothing belonging to his dead mother and his ex-wife, and jewelry, photos and letters.

When several victims disappeared while Foster was under surveillance, focus on him waned, although the Task Force continued to maintain that they were "interested" in him.

About the same time investigators cleared Ridgway, another man came under suspicion when he called the Seattle Times newspaper from the King County jail to deny he was the killer. James Daniel Davenport, 32, a former Burien-area apartment manager, was scheduled to go on trial in King County Superior Court on charges of statutory rape and indecent liberties with two 13-year-old girls. Davenport told the Times in a brief telephone conversation that when he was a taxi driver working near the Seattle-Tacoma International Airport, he saw another taxi driver kidnap a girl from Pac Highway. He said he called the Task Force with that information and offered to take a lie-detector test to verify his information. The Task Force declined.

Davenport's situation was more complicated than Foster's. Davenport, authorities confirmed, was the new identity of James

David Driggers, who had been placed in the federal witness protection program after he cooperated with the prosecution of a 1980 armed robbery. Davenport's name was one of 700 on a tip sheet at the time, according to Capt. Frank Adamson, commander of the Task Force. "That doesn't make him a suspect, but we are interested in him," Adamson said. "We are looking at a number of people in that sense, but we don't have one, two or three people that are prime suspects. We're interested in a lot of people. ... It's a big jump to be a suspect."

In 1983, two other men — Dennis Curtis Williams, 19, and David Shawn Dyer, 20, both of California — were linked together in the murder of Williams' mother. During an interview, Dyer told detectives he "hated hookers." But they, too, were dismissed.

It was time to go back to the drawing board.

In August 1984, Task Force detectives traveled to San Francisco to interview two jail inmates: Richard Carbone and Robert Matthias, who had told authorities there they were the Green River killers. Matthias said he had killed 16 women; Carbone had committed two murders with Matthias and helped him kill nine others. A few days later, Matthias admitted he and Carbone made up the stories as part of an escape attempt. He told detectives they hoped police would take them to Washington to look for the bodies of women and that they might be able to escape into the woods.

In the late spring of 1984, a reward fund established to solicit information leading to the arrest and prosecution of the Green River killer was still growing. Other rewards were also established. But no matter how many tips came in, they never led to a break in the case, and the rewards were never paid.

Police drawings of suspects in the 1980s.

The FBI
Chapter 12

THE FBI WAS INTERESTED in the Green River case from the beginning, when the first bodies were found, but kept a low profile. Officially, the Bureau had no formal role in the case until it became a matter of federal interest, that is until the crimes crossed state lines. Unofficially, the FBI was working behind the scenes, offering crime lab assistance and analysis and generally providing what was assumed, especially by the FBI, to be their greater expertise in solving such crimes.

Instead of superiority, the FBI ended up demonstrating how easily an investigation can go wrong.

In September 1982, just two months after the first bodies were found, John Douglas with the FBI's Behavioral Science Division created a 12-page profile of the probable killer. Douglas, now a retired author and expert on the criminal mind, was an FBI legend. He had worked dozens of high-profile cases around the country, and his judgment was revered.

His profile of the Green River killer has been disclosed only in parts. From what has been made public, Ridgway did fit the profile in some ways, most of them broad categories. Ridgway was white and came from a family with discord between his mother and father. He sought power and control over women. But in other ways the profile was far off the mark. It suggested that the killer was probably unemployed or chronically underemployed, an outdoorsman and in fairly good shape, despite being a drinker and a smoker. Ridgway was none of those things, except for drinking the occasional Bud Light. He was a nonsmoker with a steady job. He was relatively trim, but his primary hobbies appeared to be cruising for garage sales and prostitutes.

In 1984, the FBI also got involved in analyzing an intriguing, deceptive letter Ridgway wrote to reporter Mike Barber of the Seattle Post-Intelligencer. The letter, using bad spelling and no spaces between the words, was titled "whatyou_eedtonoaboutthegreenriverman" and was signed "callmefred." The letter enumerated 38 attributes of the Green River killer. Some were accurate. Some were designed to mislead the Task Force. The FBI examined the letter and concluded it was a fake. That was the end of the matter until years later, when Ridgway told prosecutors about the letter as part of his confession and accurately recited details. When they charged him with 48 killings, prosecutors would write of the missed opportunity: "The Task Force sent the letter to the FBI for analysis, and an 'expert' there proclaimed that the letter was not written by the killer."

In September 1984, after two years of investigation and no arrests, Washington Gov. John Spellman called for full-scale FBI assistance, and publicly criticized county officials for not calling on the FBI to take a greater role in the case, even though there was no evidence the crimes had crossed state lines. An FBI spokesman in Seattle, Joseph A. Smith Jr., temporarily settled the issue with a public statement: "There is no known interstate aspect to this matter. We can only enter a case if there is a basis for a federal investigation."

The "interstate aspect" came soon enough. In April and June 1985, bones from three women believed to be victims of the Green River killer were found near Portland, Ore., and the FBI had its official entree. By January 1986, another 10 FBI agents hit town to help the investigation, bringing the number of agents working the case to 14, and the total Task Force number to 56. Also in January, Task Force commander Frank Adamson announced the killer would be caught that year. He said he was being more optimistic than predictive, but the FBI activity had reporters on edge. With the entry of the FBI and the new agents, rumors were rife that something was about to break. The FBI had the same feeling, and promptly zeroed in on a person of interest.

Out of the Task Force's catalog of 12,000 names, including several considered genuine possibilities, the FBI focused on Ernest W. "Bill" McLean, a trapper who lived in Riverton Heights, not far from the Pac Highway.

McLean didn't fit the FBI profile very well, either. He was an outdoorsman, and he knew the Green River and rural areas of King County, but he didn't drink or smoke, and he didn't frequent prostitutes. Nevertheless, the FBI picked him up on Feb. 6, 1986, in what appeared to be the break everyone anticipated. Neighbors called a local television station to let them know the FBI had arrested the Green River killer. McLean's name quickly went public.

At his arrest, McLean appeared to confirm the authorities' suspicions with what has to be one of the oddest and most damning statements ever made by an innocent man: "What took you so long?" With that, FBI agents thought they had their man.

They searched his house, but found nothing of value. They also collected samples of saliva and head and pubic hair from both McLean and his wife. Then, after 11 hours of questioning and numerous polygraphs, McLean was released. With his reputation ruined, he, too, had become a victim of the Green River killer and promptly sued both the county and the Seattle Post-Intelligencer. Those cases were later settled out of court.

The following month, fresh from being burned by the McLean arrest, the FBI shifted its focus to Ridgway.

The truck painter had passed a polygraph test in May 1984, but he had come back under suspicion through Rebecca Garde Guay, a prostitute who telephoned the Task Force in November 1984 to tell them about an assault by a john in November 1982. Her story is recounted in court papers in a section called "The victim who escaped."

Guay had been reluctant to talk to investigators because it also implicated her in criminal activity. But after hearing about the murders for more than two years, she came forward and told her story. She had been hitchhiking, standing at a bus stop along Pac Highway near South 200th Street, when a man drove up in a maroon Dodge pickup truck with a black canopy. He was feeling a bit down. He admitted he had been arrested in a prostitution sting. The courts were trying to take away his son, Matthew. Everyone, he told Guay, was out to get him that day. The sympathy factor worked.

Guay agreed to a $20 car date and directed him to South 204th just off the Strip. He wanted her to go into the woods. She agreed, walking several yards behind him. She caught up with him on a steep incline. His shorts were down around his tennis shoes and knee-high socks. The deep woods were dark in the late-afternoon sun. She kept her clothes on and dropped to her knees in front of the man, who, she told police, never did get an erection. Then he started yelling at Guay, claiming she bit him. He put her in a police-style chokehold. She managed to turn over on her back. She feared he was going to kill her.

In between gasps for air, she pleaded for her life. His grip loosened slightly and she escaped. He stood there in a daze, his shorts still around his knee-highs and tennis shoes. She never saw the man again, but her description of the man and the truck fit Ridgway. When shown a photographic montage of six men, she immediately identified Ridgway as the attacker.

The story eventually made its way to the FBI, but it took months.

Initially, Guay's report was investigated by a Task Force detective, who brought Ridgway in for an interview on Feb. 23, 1985. Ridgway waived his right to have a lawyer present. He told the detective that he had picked up Guay in his maroon pickup and acknowledged that they struck a deal for him to pay her $20 for oral sex. He also admitted choking her, but said he had a reason. She had bit him during the act, and he choked her for 10 to 15 seconds in retaliation. All he remembered saying to her was, "You bit me." Guay ran to a nearby trailer. Ridgway pulled up his shorts and left.

Ridgway appeared to be fully cooperative. It was disarming. He would admit everything he thought the Task Force already knew about him and then add a little more. The detective's interest in Ridgway was piqued, and he recommended reopening the Ridgway file. It was assigned to longtime Task Force and King County police investigator Jim Doyon. Doyon was sent out of state before he could investigate Ridgway, and the file was then turned over to two FBI agents. They promptly invited Ridgway in for an interview.

On March 17, 1986, Ridgway appeared voluntarily at the Burien precinct offices. Not bringing a lawyer along helped dampen suspicion. He again admitted choking Guay but embellished his story to say she had bitten hard enough to draw blood. Of course he had never done anything like that before, he told them. Then it occurred to him. He had choked his ex-wife Marcia Winslow, and he thought she might have reported it to the police. So he told them about that, too.

The agents pressed him about his interaction with prostitutes. Warming to the topic and appearing to want to help, he said he hadn't been "dating" for a year and half because of the Green River killings and the fact that he had contracted venereal disease at least 15 times. Instead, he had taken to picking up prostitutes in his vehicle only to talk to them.

He told the FBI he was a fisherman and fished both the Green River and several lakes in Eastern Washington. At the end of the interview, the agents asked Ridgway if he would take another lie-detector test, this time from the FBI. He had passed the one in 1984, and he agreed to take another. They set an appointment three days later, on March 20.

On that date, attorney David Middaugh called the FBI agent and said he was representing Ridgway. There would be no lie-detector test. Middaugh also demanded that there be no more interviews by the FBI. There are few details in the court record that explain the FBI's actions. But the FBI backed off, and the Ridgway file was once again declared inactive. Furthermore, the FBI began reducing its involvement with the Task Force.

By April, only eight FBI agents remained assigned to the case, and the Task Force began to shrink. By August, only six FBI agents remained. By September 1986, the county joined in the cutback, trimming the Task Force down to 20. Adamson, who had led the Task Force since its inception, left to take charge of the Maple Valley precinct that served southeast King County.

Ridgway got away again.

Jim Bates
Stevie Hartley reads during a sit-in at Task Force headquarters in July 1986.

Impatience
Chapter 13

ON MAY 26, 1984, THREE YOUTHS found the remains of Colleen Renee Brockman in a ditch along Jovita Boulevard, a winding rural road more than 20 miles south of Seattle near Sumner. Colleen died so young — at the age of 15 — that she still wore braces. Her body had been in the ditch for more than a year, and if there were other identifying characteristics, they were long gone. A month after her remains were found, Colleen was still unidentified; one more nameless victim of the Green River killer.

In June, Colleen's father, Barry Brockman, read a news report about the body, noted the braces, and wondered if it could be his daughter, a frequent runaway who had become involved in prostitution. Colleen's family last saw her two days before Christmas 1982. The next day, on Christmas Eve, Ridgway had picked up Colleen in downtown Seattle, north of Chinatown, and killed her in the back of his truck. As she struggled and begged for her life, Ridgway used a ruse he had developed for victims like her. "Don't fight," he told her. "I'll let you go." That allowed him to put his foot into her neck and finish the job. Ridgway then drove down to Jovita Boulevard and dumped Colleen's body near a creek about 20 feet off the road. In June 2003, Ridgway was able to direct detectives to within 150 feet of where he had dumped her body almost 20 years earlier.

Most of Gary Ridgway's victims were involved in prostitution, but most of them were also children. Of the first two dozen confirmed victims of the Green River killer, 19 were teenagers, many of them just 15 or 16. Colleen Brockman had no criminal record. She didn't show up on police background checks. By many measures, she was like thousands of other girls her age, and the accumulation of such stories was beginning to have an effect.

In the mid-1980s, public pressure to solve the Green River case began to build. Critics complained that not enough was being done to find the killer. Some suggested that police weren't working the case as hard as they would if the victims were from prominent families, or if they were college students. A social worker at Harborview Medical Center in Seattle said the level of investigation merely reflected the community's level of interest in the slaying of prostitutes, and a growing core of advocates set out to change that.

In November 1984, KIRO-TV joined the cause, offering a $100,000 reward for information leading to the capture of the Green River killer. The Highline Community Council also offered a reward, this one for $28,381. In April 1985, a group of vocal Christians marched down the Sea-Tac Strip, where many of the Green River victims had disappeared, to show support and offer prayers for the Green River Task Force. As one man marched, he carried a huge wooden cross. Marchers said that during the time of the murders and the discovery of the bodies, churches had failed to get out and pray for a stop to the killings.

In July 1985, on the third anniversary of the discovery of the first victims, women gathered for vigils in Seattle, San Francisco and Vancouver, B.C. Cookie Hunt, a spokeswoman for the Women's Coalition to Stop the Green River Murders, said the commemorations were intended to remind people that the dozens of unsolved murders represented the universal problem of violence against women. Women who knew the victims were encouraged to speak about them and how they felt about the case. Members said the names of 80 other missing or dead women should be added to the list of possible Green River victims. A handful of women also marched in front of the King County Courthouse, demanding increased efforts to capture the Green River killer. Hunt criticized the Green River Task Force for working "9-to-5 hours" and asked for a stop on arrests of prostitutes until the killer was caught. She said the county was putting too much attention on curbing prostitution and not enough on finding the killer.

In July 1986, the start of the fifth year of the investigation, a panel of university professors and journalists rated the Green River serial murder case as one of the most overlooked stories by the national media the previous year. It was rated 24th among stories that got less coverage than they deserved. The coordinator of the rankings said national publications and television networks ignored the case out of personal bias, because most of the victims were prostitutes, because some were black and because Seattle was a distant, relatively small city.

Also that July, about a dozen members of the Women's Coalition to Stop the Green River Murders held a two-day sit-in at the headquarters of the Task Force, calling for a more thorough review of the evidence and opposing plans to reduce funding. They maintained the vigil for 46 hours, symbolic of the presumed number of Green River victims at that time. A demonstration was scheduled to coincide with the fourth anniversary of the first discovery of a Green River victim.

Mary Ellen Stone of the King County Sexual Assault Center remembers the time well: There was an attitude of, "Well, it's not me" or anyone I know, she said. She described it as a "sleazy" time, when people thought of prostitutes and street people as disposable elements of society.

Stone also remembers thinking the case would never be solved. It had been so long and it didn't seem there were any solid leads. For the next 15 years, she was right.

•••

The year 1986 was a turning point for the Green River Task Force. The year started in January with Capt. Frank Adamson, who now had 55 investigators on the case, predicting that this would be the year the Green River killer is caught. Weeks later, it looked like that had happened, with the highly publicized arrest of E.W. McLean. It soon became clear that they had the wrong man, and in addition to a lawsuit and settlement, there was a political fallout. Angered by the arrests and media circus, members of the King County Council questioned the amount of staff time and money being spent. The Task Force was trimmed from 55 investigators to 47.

As the year progressed, Adamson and the Task Force continued to take heat from all sides. In September, a dozen investigators were reassigned to other duties, and County Executive Tim Hill and Sheriff Vern Thomas announced that there would be more cuts to come. When the media reported that the county intended to reduce the Task Force to 20 investigators, the news prompted another wave of protests questioning the county's commitment to solving the case.

In October, Adamson submitted to a full hour of questions and criticism from the Women's Coalition to Stop the Green River Murders at a forum held at the Seattle Public Library. Many of the questions dealt with budget cuts, with Adamson put in the position of defending county policy even though he and other Task Force members had opposed the cuts. Critics also took jabs at the Task Force for failing to find the killer and suggested that budget cuts showed they weren't serious about solving the case. It was a low point for Adamson. "The Task Force cares," he told the crowd. "It's sad that people don't realize that."

Elsewhere, there was apathy. There had been no disappearances linked to the case for two years, and public interest was starting to fade. Prostitutes were returning to the Strip. "I'm not afraid any more," said a woman who preferred to be known as Tina. "There haven't been any girls found dead for a long time." King County police were now making about 10 prostitution arrests a month. "They're coming back faster than we can arrest them," said King County Police Maj. Raymond Jenne. "I think the fear has gone away."

By late 1986, the FBI also cut back, withdrawing 10 agents, and by the end of the year, Hill announced that the Task Force would be cut again, down to 12. In an interview late that year, shortly before his own departure, Adamson was reflective. "These people are very dedicated," he said of the reassigned investigators. "It's hard for them to walk away from this investigation and turn their work over to someone else."

Gary Ridgway: The Green River Killer 83

Wendy
Coffield

Debra Lynn
Bonner

Duane Hamamura
City of Kent police Officer Randy Bourne walks toward three Kent firefighters as they remove the body of Wendy Coffield from the Green River on July 15, 1982. Ever since, Coffield has been known as the first official victim of the Green River killer.

Cathy Stone
Marine Patrol divers recover Debra Lynn Bonner's body from the Green River. On shore are King County Police Detectives Dave Reichert, center left, and Earl Tripp, center right.

Gary Ridgway's family home. In 1960, his parents, Thomas and Mary Ridgway, purchased this house at 4404 S. 175th St. in McMicken Heights, now a part of the city of SeaTac.

Washington State Archives

Gary Ridgway lived at this home at 21859 32nd Place S. in SeaTac from January 1982 until August 1989. Many of his victims were killed in this house.

Dean Forbes

Gary Kissel

A prostitute works the Strip on a rainy day in the 1980s.

Gary Ridgway: The Green River Killer   85

Kelly Marie Ware

Mark Morris
The remains of Kelly Marie Ware were found near South 192nd Street, just south of Sea-Tac Airport, on Oct. 29, 1983.

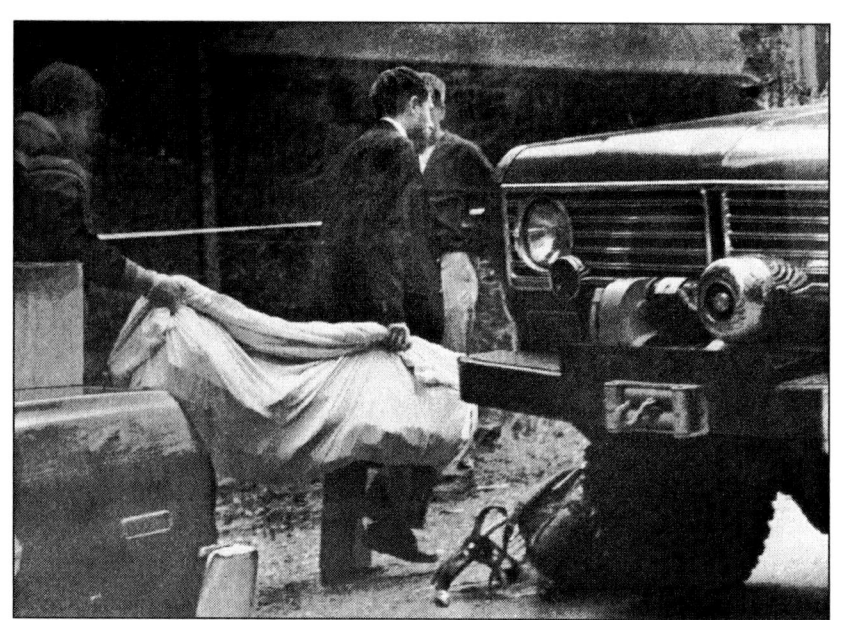

Steve Botkin
Bill Haglund of the King County Medical Examiner's office, center, helps carry one of two bodies discovered on April 1, 1984, near Star Lake Road. The two bodies were later identified as Terry Rene Milligan and Sandra K Gabbert.

Terry Rene Milligan

Sandra K Gabbert

86 Gary Ridgway: The Green River Killer

Jim Bates
Psychic Barbara Kubik Patten on May 7, 1984, the same day Gary Ridgway took a polygraph test.

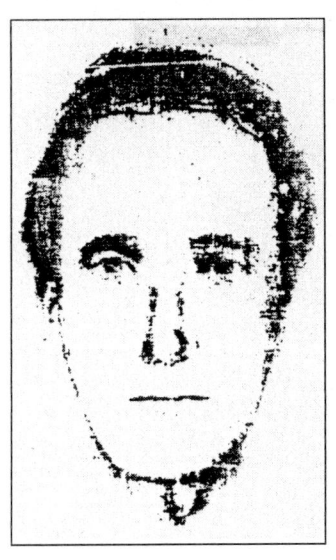

Psychic Barbara Kubik Patten sketched what she calls her mystery man, with whom she spoke at a fast food restaurant in October 1982. She said independent extrasensory perceptions suggested the killer's name was a variant of Richard, such as Richardson.

Gary Ridgway: The Green River Killer   87

Mike Doll with Pierce County Search & Rescue looks for more bones on Mountain View Drive. In January 1986 some remains were found just south of Auburn's Mountain View Cemetery.

Ralph Radford

Ralph Radford
Shari Bennecke gets ready for a search along Highway 410 in December 1984.

Jim Bates
Explorer Search & Rescue volunteers gathered March 14, 1985, to search near Star Lake Road, where four days earlier the remains of Carrie A. Rois were found.

Carrie A. Rois

Ralph Radford
Golznia Nickals protests and hands out literature on the unsolved Green River killings on July 15, 1985.

Gary Ridgway: The Green River Killer 89

Jeff Franko
Dick McNeely leads a group of citizens in a march down the Sea-Tac Strip in April 1985. The group offered prayers in support of the Green River Task Force.

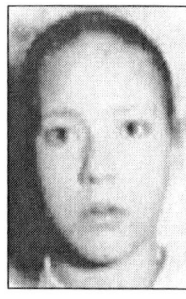

Cheryl Wims, 18, disappeared from Seattle in May 1983. When her remains were found in March of 1984, north of Sea-Tac Airport, authorities released this artificial reconstruction of her face in hope of identifying the remains.

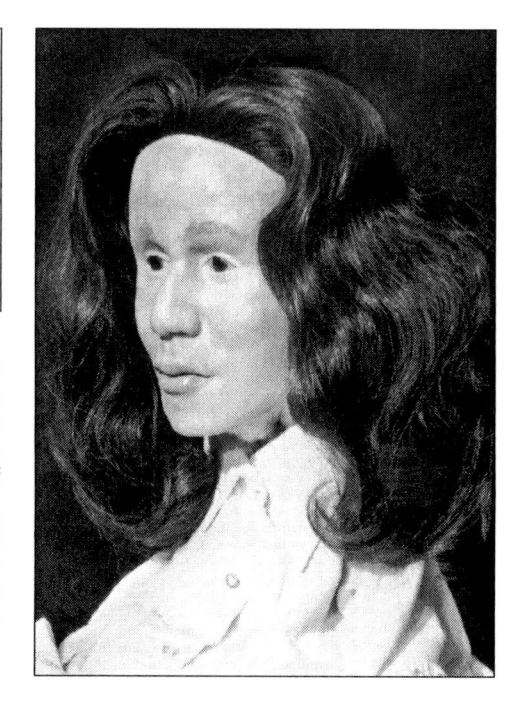

90   Gary Ridgway: The Green River Killer

A member of the Green River Task Force works beneath a chart of the then-known victims and missing women, right.

In July 1986 Sally Nipertia, below, enters tips into Green River Task Force's computer database.

Ralph Radford

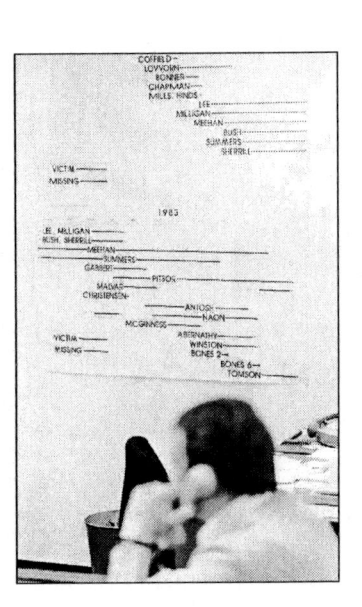

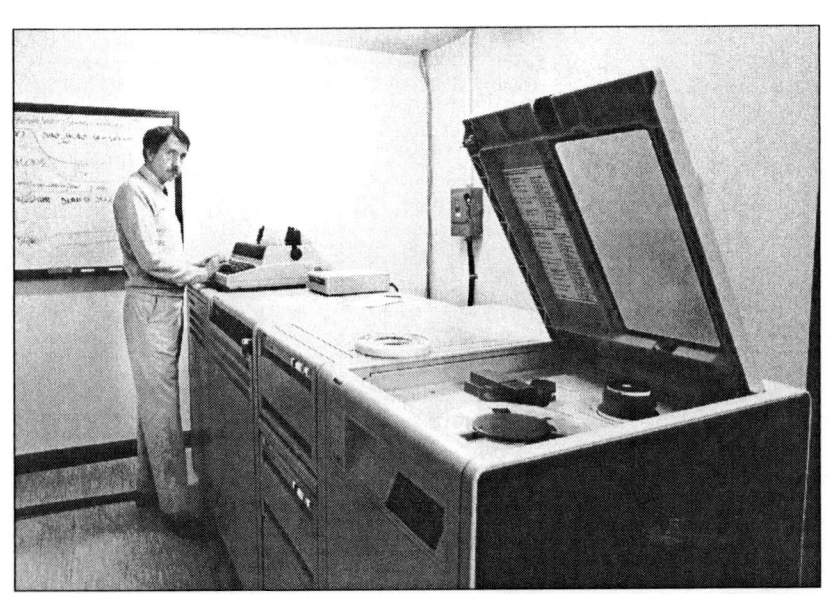

Peter Haley
Police Lt. Dan Nolan at the Task Force's main computer.

Gary Ridgway: The Green River Killer 91

Ralph Radford
Unidentified remains were found near this car off of Mountain View Drive in December 1985.

Ralph Radford
Fae Brooks, Green River Task Force spokeswoman, speaks with KOMO-TV reporter Keith Eldridge, center, and other media at a victim dump site in January 1986.

Lisa Yates

Jim Hallas

Search & rescue teams converge at a base camp where the remains of Lisa Yates, 19, were found on March 13, 1984. The site was about 5 miles east of North Bend along Interstate 90.

Jim Bates

Members of the Green River Task Force attend a briefing in January 1984, shortly after the group was expanded to 36 full-time investigators.

Gary Ridgway: The Green River Killer 93

Marcus R.Donner
In 1992 Green River Task Force Detectives Thomas Jensen and James Doyon stand with file cabinets containing 50,000 pages of tips.

Marcus R.Donner
Robert Keppel, chief criminal investigator for the Attorney General's office, became a renowned expert on serial murder.

Denise Bush

Marcus R.Donner
Explorer Scouts from the Olympia area help search a site in Tukwila where the remains of Denise Bush were found in February 1990.

The Kenworth Truck Co. complex in Renton where Gary Ridgway worked when he was arrested.

Patrick Hagerty

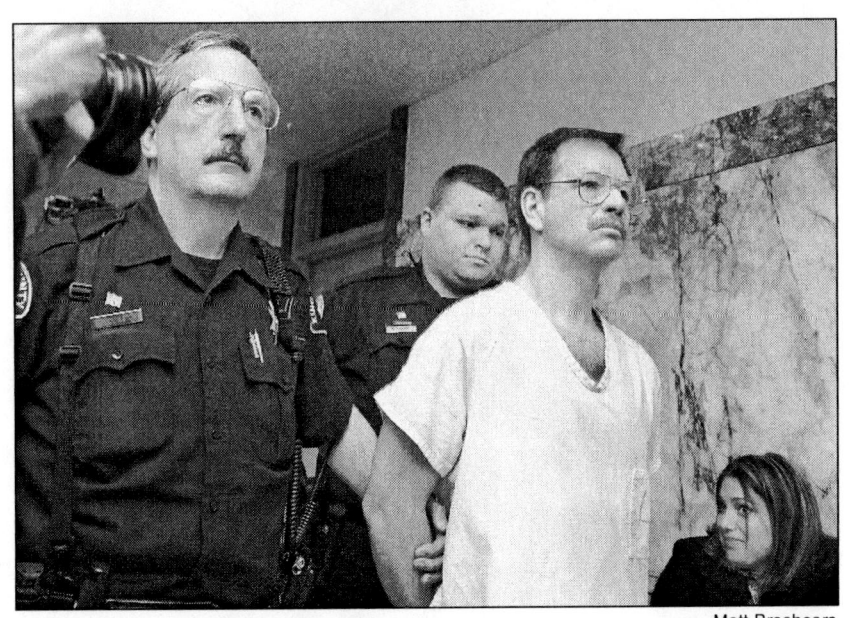

Matt Brashears
Green River killer Gary Ridgway is led into the courtroom April 15, 2002, when prosecutors announced they will seek the death penalty in his trial.

Tim Meehan, the brother of Mary Meehan, said that although Ridgway wasn't charged with his sister's death, he believes Ridgway is responsible.

Matt Brashears

Gary Ridgway: The Green River Killer 95

King County Prosecutor Norm Maleng on Dec. 5, 2001, announces four charges of aggravated murder against Green River suspect Gary Ridgway in a packed press conference.

Gary Ridgway's childhood home was searched after his arrest.

96　　　　　Gary Ridgway: The Green River Killer

A Washington State Crime Lab technician examines the kitchen in a south Des Moines home, formerly owned by Ridgway, searching for any clues after Ridgway's arrest.

David Nelson

Gary Kissel

After Gary Ridgway's arrest, investigators dug up the lawn of the home on Auburn's West Hill, where he was living with his wife, Judith.

Gary Ridgway: The Green River Killer   97

Patrick Hagerty
A detective with the Task Force places a bone fragment into an evidence bag held by Dr. Kathy Taylor of the King County Medical Examiner's office on Aug. 23, 2003, in a wooded area off the Kent/Des Moines Road. Human bone fragments found over three days have not been identified.

Trying to avoid the death penalty, Gary Ridgway in the summer of 2003 led investigators to sites where years earlier he had left bodies.

Green River Task Force

Matt Brashears

The Green River Task Force found the remains of Marie Malvar in a wooded ravine in the 29200 block of 65th Avenue South in Auburn on Sept. 28 and 29, 2003.

Marie Malvar

Gary Ridgway: The Green River Killer 99

Green River Task Force investigators, from left to right, Sue Peters, Jon Mattsen, Randy Mullinax and Tom Jensen talk about spending weeks interrogating Gary Ridgway in this room. Ridgway sat in the hard plastic chair at left of the table.

Rick Schweinhart

Matt Brashears
King County Sheriff's Office spokesman Sgt. John Urquhart stands next to a wall of boxed evidence in a secure warehouse in South Seattle. Behind him, on the top shelf, is evidence from the Green River killer investigation in the 1980s.

Sheriff Dave Reichert watches as Gary Ridgway pleads guilty to 48 counts of murder on Nov. 5, 2003.

Elaine Thompson

Maxwell Balmain
A heavy guard of officers takes serial killer Gary Ridgway down a hallway after his confession in court on Nov. 5, 2003.

Gary Kissel
Debra York, the aunt of Green River murder victim Cynthia Hinds, is comforted by Deniece Griffin after Gary Ridgway pleaded guilty to 48 counts of murder. Griffin was a friend of Hinds and Opal Mills.

King County Detective Ross Nooney and Sgt. Frank Atchley at a search of Ridgway's home in 1987.

A Suspect Again
Chapter 14

A PROSTITUTE PUT GARY RIDGWAY back on the Task Force's radar in the summer of 1986. He would shortly become their leading suspect.

The development came just as the Green River Task Force faced a crossroads in its four-year history. Victims of the killer now totaled 36, and the case was still unsolved. A panel of high-ranking county police officials had began a review on June 1 to determine whether money and manpower for the investigative unit should increase, be cut or stay the same. Though aware of growing frustration and criticism, Green River Task Force detectives kept focused on the case, reviewing old information, collating new data and looking for connections that might lead them to the killer.

On Aug. 12, 1986, detectives contacted Paige Miley, who had a history of prostitution in the area. They were looking into the death of Kim Nelson, whose skeletal remains were discovered off Interstate 90 near North Bend two months earlier. It was a dump site for the killer. Two other victims were found in that same area. Nelson, 20, was a striking, 6-foot-tall blonde, with short bleached hair. Miley briefly worked the Strip with her during 1983. She had a very interesting story for detectives.

More than two years earlier, on Oct. 30, 1983, Nelson was released from the King County Jail and joined up with Miley. Together with their pimps, they all stayed at the Ben Carol Motel at South 144th and Pac Highway for two nights. During the night the women looked for johns at the Evergreen Truck Stop at South 348th Street, near Pac Highway. By day, they stayed in their room.

On Nov. 1, 1983, they decided to work Pac Highway to make rent money. They left their room at 11 a.m. and went to a covered bus stop at South 144th Street and Pac Highway. Miley picked up a quick car date. When she returned 15 to 20 minutes later, Nelson was gone. It was the first time they had been on Pac Highway together and the first time she knew of Nelson working there, but Nelson's disappearance didn't bother Miley too much. The life of a street prostitute is unpredictable. Still, she was aware that someone was killing prostitutes. The newspapers kept the story alive.

Several nights later Miley was working the same general area alone when a man in a red pickup truck, with a cab-over canopy, approached. The man was in his late 20s or early 30s with brown hair and a wispy mustache. He wore a plaid shirt, jeans and a baseball cap with writing on it. Between his legs he held a can of Budweiser beer. After talking about a date, the man asked where her tall blonde friend was. Miley's street experience sent up a warning flag. The only time he could have seen her together with Nelson was the morning when Nelson disappeared.

After Miley's 1986 interview with police, she saw the possible connection with the Green River killer. She assisted a police artist in drawing the man in the red pickup. Detectives couldn't help but notice that he looked like Ridgway. Detectives reviewing Ridgway's case also noticed that during a 1984 interview with Ridgway, he said he had seen Nelson on South 144th, but hadn't talked to her. He did say he had talked to Nelson's "roommate." Later, as the investigation into Ridgway progressed, Miley picked Ridgway out of a photo-montage as the man who asked her about Nelson.

Ridgway had been cleared by the 1984 lie-detector test, but Miley's story was too incriminating to ignore. The case against Ridgway was officially reopened on Aug. 19, 1986. Detectives embarked on a number of interviews of Ridgway's ex-wives and former girlfriends. They heard stories of kinky sex, his venereal diseases, assaults, outdoor sex, his penchant for prostitutes, his pickup trucks. Had they found the Green River killer?

A number of other prostitutes and pimps who knew victims had already provided tantalizing stories that linked Ridgway to their disappearances. Task force detectives searched them out again. They found Cynthia Bassett-Ornelas. On March 3, 1983, she and Alma Anne Smith, 18, of Lynnwood, were working dates outside the Red Lion Inn at South 188th Street and Pac Highway. Smith, a blonde, disappeared that night. She was found April 2, 1984, near Star Lake, where five other bodies of Green River victims eventually were found. Now, three years after Smith's disappearance, detectives showed Ornelas a photo-montage of six men. Ornelas picked out Ridgway as looking like the man she had seen sitting in a blue/white pickup at the Red Lion. Smith had left in that truck earlier and never returned.

She remembered the man because he tried to date her, too. And because he asked about her "blonde girlfriend." The man spooked her, and she turned him down. She said the driver looked like Ridgway but had "longer, thinner hair and thinner lips." She couldn't positively say Ridgway was the driver. Ridgway would later confirm that was the night he tried to kill two women, one after another. After Ornelas refused him, he was unable to find another victim that evening.

A blue and white pickup truck similar to the one Ornelas had seen at the Red Lion March 3 had been reported to police by Curtis Weaver. On April 10, 1983, Weaver saw his girlfriend, Gail Mathews, get in the truck and he never saw her again. Her body was found five months later.

Detectives decided it was time to camp on Ridgway. He needed to be followed. Perhaps he would lead them to a dumping ground for bodies. Maybe he would take them nowhere.

From Oct. 9 to Oct. 24, 1986, detectives set up surveillance on Ridgway. He worked the second shift at the Kenworth Truck Co. plant on East Marginal Way in Seattle, and was expected at work by 3:40 p.m. when his shift started. Often he left home hours before his shift. Detectives also occasionally watched him after he left work at 12:10 a.m.

Ridgway obviously knew his way around Pac Highway and its environs. He cruised the highway often and parked in areas where prostitution was a daily occurrence. Two Pac Highway locations where he parked — Larry's Market at South 144th Street and a 7-Eleven store at South 142nd Street — were locations from which eight Green River victims had disappeared. On one occasion during the surveillance, he drove back and forth two times on Rainier Avenue South between Seward Park Drive and Andover Street. Four victims had disappeared from that area. Ridgway drove well below the legal limit and kept his attention focused on what was happening along the side of the streets and on sidewalks. Often he would suddenly turn onto a side street, turn around and then proceed in the opposite direction for no apparent reason.

Ridgway was definitely a "person of interest" as the Task Force referred to people who may or may not be suspects. Investigators didn't feel they had enough to arrest him yet, but he was back in their crosshairs. Detectives had closely watched Ridgway early in their investigation and did an intensive background check, including studying his daily work records for the years 1982-1984, his gas credit card and bank records for the same period of time, and interviewing friends and associates. They could find nothing that would exclude him as a suspect. It was time to take the next step.

In April 1987, they obtained a search warrant for Ridgway's house, his vehicles and his body. "It is highly possible that Gary Leon Ridgway is the Green River killer," Detective Matthew Haney wrote in asking for the warrant. "Even though the times of day, and days of the week (when victims disappeared) have varied greatly, detectives were unable to eliminate Ridgway from the 29 most accurately known missing dates and times."

The April 8 search caught neighbors by surprise. During interviews at the time, they described Ridgway as a nice guy who got upset when kids threatened to harm an animal. One neighbor even let his girlfriend's pregnant daughter live with Ridgway. Police tried to keep the search low-key and referred to Ridgway as a "person of interest," fearing a media circus similar to the one that surrounded the search of McLean's house about a year earlier. But reporters and photographers camped out in Ridgway's neighborhood for much of the day.

Detectives were looking for the tools of a killer — ligatures for strangling and binding material for control — and for souvenirs from a kill, such as toenails or jewelry. Sometimes killers keep a log or tape recording, and sexual devices such as handcuffs and vibrators. At Ridgway's home detectives found maps of Seattle, Washington and Oregon, clear plastic, rope and spray paint. They cut test samples from his carpet. They collected vacuum cleaner bags, VHS tapes, a piece of jewelry with a broken turquoise stone. The same day, detectives conducted a search of Ridgway's body. They picked up Ridgway at Kenworth and took him to an undisclosed location. There, Ridgway pulled out chest, stomach and pubic hairs. He removed hair samples from the front, top, right and left sides and back of his scalp. A detective cut hairs from the same places on his head. And he bit down on a piece of gauze to provide saliva — and cells, which contain DNA unique to each individual.

Detectives also searched his vehicles and his work locker at the truck plant on East Marginal Way. They took wrenches, a white carpenter's apron, a pair of paper coveralls, a pair of used blue coveralls with "Gary" written on them in red, food, many pieces of plastic sheeting, eyeglasses, paper cups and notebooks. They found a pamphlet about marijuana. After his arrest in November 2001, Ridgway told detectives that he didn't use alcohol much, claiming that the only drug he ever used was marijuana and that rarely.

Ridgway had killed women — many, many women — in that house and truck. Those killed in the house had been carried through the living room and out the front door, placed in the back of the pickup and driven to dump sites. But the Washington State Patrol Crime Lab was unable to find a single piece of evidence that connected Ridgway to any of those murders. The lab didn't attempt to do a DNA profile of Ridgway using the gauze chew, because the technology simply wasn't available. That evidence was put into cold storage, together with traces of semen that had been removed about five years earlier from victims dumped in or beside the Green River. That evidence would all wait, not forgotten, for 14 years. Detectives knew that someday, when science advanced far enough, the DNA might solve the case.

The 1987 search warrant was sealed — not available to the press and public — because witnesses named in the warrant, including ex-wives and girlfriends, feared for their lives. Ridgway's violent streak was well-known to prosecutors. Information in the warrant also revealed details about Ridgway that investigators claimed could harm the investigation if they became public. The full report would not be unsealed until after Ridgway's arrest in 2001.

Ridgway's notoriety among friends and co-workers grew. They whispered about the police suspicions, and even jokingly called him Green River Gary. He took it in good humor. No one else was killed in 1987, at least as far as investigators know, and the remains of the last known victim of the killer — Cindy Anne Smith — were found on June 27, 1987. Feeling safe again, prostitutes returned to the Strip. Families continued to wake up to days filled with grief.

Cindy Anne's killer, meanwhile, was in a relationship that would lead to marriage in 1988. This time Ridgway's intended was Judith L. Lynch, who was five years his senior. She was to be a June bride.

The couple met in February 1985, and Lynch moved into Ridgway's house several months later. She has never spoken publicly about Ridgway, her relationship with him or what she either knew or may have suspected about her husband. How Ridgway explained to Judith why he was a suspect or why they searched his house isn't known. What is known is that she stayed with him and agreed to marry him.

First, they needed a minister and a place to hold the wedding. A phone book provided the first, and a neighbor the second. The big day was June 12, 1988, at 2 p.m. Ridgway paid $40 to Ellis Forsman, the minister at the Seatac Church of Christ, to perform the ceremony. His money was really a donation to help the less fortunate in the area. There was nothing remarkable about the Ridgways or the outdoor ceremony to spark a memory for Forsman years later. For sure, Ridgway wasn't a member of Forsman's congregation.

About six months after Ridgway's third and final wedding, Green River investigators turned to a national TV audience in hopes of finding a killer.

Duane Hamamura
An appliance salesperson watches 'Manhunt'on Dec. 7, 1988.

The Manhunt
Chapter 15

TRUE AND UNSOLVED CRIME was the reality television craze of 1988, with "America's Most Wanted" and "Unsolved Mysteries" heading the list. Viewers seemed especially drawn to shows that invited them to become personally involved in fighting crime through toll-free tip lines, and Geraldo Rivera, then a TV promoter and producer, was eager to give them more of what they wanted. Rivera pitched a TV special to the Green River Task Force, but King County officials turned him down. "We were afraid it might come off as Geraldo-esque," said Task Force Cmdr. Maj. Robert Evans. But Evans eventually changed his mind after seeing other television shows with tip-lines leading to arrests.

It wasn't as though the Task Force had a shortage of potential suspects. In fact, it already had thousands. Some were tips from local residents. Others were culled from lists of men convicted of violent crimes against women. What surprised even Task Force members were the numbers of men out there with records of assault, rape, kidnapping and other crimes of violence most often directed at women. Task Force members also were coming up with their own lists of most likely suspects. But so far, they all seemed to be dead ends.

You go to one detective's desk, said Task Force Lt. Dan Nolan, and he'll have a half-dozen names and he'll swear one of them is the killer. Go to the next desk a couple of feet away, Nolan said, and that guy will have 10 different names and he'll swear up and down that one of them has got to be the Green River killer — and both of them can give you lots of good reasons why.

County officials also were under mounting public pressure. The Seattle Times newspaper had run a six-part series detailing what the newspaper reported were several missed opportunities to catch the killer.

Evans and county officials agreed to a local production company's offer to produce a TV special hosted by actor Patrick Duffy. It would focus on the Green River case, as well as unsolved serial murders in San Diego and elsewhere across the nation. A call-in tip line would offer a $100,000 reward for information leading to the arrest and prosecution of the Green River killer.

With Crime Stoppers and other groups underwriting costs, production crews went to work in the summer of 1988. That same summer Gary Ridgway and his new wife, Judith, were living in the small rambler on 32nd Place South near South 200th Street. Less than a quarter mile to the west was Pacific Highway South. A few miles north, crews were shooting location shots for the upcoming television special, using actresses to play prostitutes for some atmosphere shots.

During July and August, Task Force members also were swapping notes with detectives in San Diego, where police were investigating the serial murders of 34 women since 1984. Nearly all the San Diego victims had ties to prostitution, drugs and street life. But like other serial cases, no ties to the Green River deaths were ever found.

The Task Force announced the planned television special in September. Evans, who gave approval for the television special, couldn't help but wonder if he made the right call. A reporter asked if Evans thought the special could solve the case. "If this doesn't work, I'm going to be the biggest ass ever in all law enforcement," he said.

The two-hour special, "Manhunt ... Live: A Chance to End the Nightmare," was nationally broadcast twice on the night of Dec. 7. Viewed by an estimated 50 million viewers in the U.S. and Canada, the show painted a picture of Pacific Highway South near Sea-Tac Airport that drew hoots from some locals. The opening sequence featured shots of bars and neon signs and supposed prostitutes and johns, with the seaminess exaggerated for dramatic effect. A narrator solemnly intoned, "The Sea-Tac Strip. Two miles of honky-tonks and hookers. Drugs. Teenage sex for sale."

Host Patrick Duffy talked about the Green River and other cases. He repeatedly implored viewers to call the 1-800 tip line, staffed by a bank of 70 police officers and investigators. The calls immediately began, hundreds before the first commercial. The hosts breathlessly reported: "A man has just called us with information about a man now living in San Diego who used to live in Kent where the first five Green River victims were found!"

Patrons at the Denny's restaurant on South 188th Street near the airport watched the show on the television over the bar, expressing varying degrees of interest. "I don't know, man, it's been six years," one man snorted. Who's going to watch a television show and suddenly remember somebody they saw doing something suspicious four or five years ago? he asked. Seattle salesman Tom Edwards approved of the Hollywood strategy, saying it might jog somebody's memory. "I think they should have done this years ago," Edwards added.

Near the end of the show, King County homicide detective Dave Reichert looked into the camera and said he had a message for the Green River killer: "You know I've worked this case for six years now, and I feel very confident someone will be leading us to you. When we get this information, no one will care anything about you or your problems. Many investigators believe you enjoy the killings. Several of us believe that you are haunted by them, that you want your own nightmare to stop. You must contact me soon. If we identify you first, no one will care what you think or feel. It will be too late. Please call me."

After Reichert's plea, a man claiming to be the killer did call. When the show was rerun later in the evening, complete with updates, Reichert said he talked to the man but wasn't sure if the caller was the real killer. It wasn't the real killer, of course, just one of thousands of tips that led nowhere.

The toll-free tip line for "Manhunt ... Live" remained open to callers for several weeks after the broadcast. The Task Force counted more than 1,500 potential leads from more than 16,000 calls nationwide offering tips in the Green River case. Not every call generated a "tip sheet," said Task Force Sgt. Bruce Peterson. "We're not taking down information from somebody who calls up and says the Republican Party is responsible," Peterson said. "We got one of those."

Some of the telephone tips provided the name of William Jay Stevens II of Spokane. Stevens was on the list of more than 12,000 names already compiled by Task Force members over the years. His name was added because he once broke into a business that sells law enforcement equipment. It was long speculated the Green River killer might be somebody posing as a cop. Stevens' whereabouts had been unknown since 1981, when he fled a work-release program while serving a sentence for the burglary. Tips to "Manhunt ... Live" helped the Task Force locate him in an unexpected setting — law school.

The 38-year-old Stevens was now a popular student at the Gonzaga University School of Law in Spokane and was close to obtaining his degree. Task force members during the closing weeks of 1988 learned Stevens had made numerous trips to the Seattle area during the mid-1980s. He collected police equipment and owned a number of vehicles, including a police car that was surplused by a department and sold at auction.

Stevens was arrested at his Spokane home Jan. 9, 1989, on a fugitive warrant for fleeing a work-release program. A search of his home turned up police equipment and badges, along with a Seattle police uniform. There were dozens of handguns, including a .44-Magnum revolver Stevens later claimed once belonged to actor Clint Eastwood and was used in the movie, "Dirty Harry." Task force members discovered Stevens was a packrat who carried boxes of maps, old newspapers, credit-card receipts and his police gear as he moved from place to place during his seven years as a fugitive in the 1980s. He made frequent trips to the Seattle area and Spokane while living in the Portland, Ore., area, where four victims linked to the Green River case were found.

While he was the focus of months of intense scrutiny, Stevens never was arrested in any of the Green River deaths. He was first held in custody to complete the sentence from his 1981 burglary conviction in King County. Then he was arrested and held by federal authorities for investigation of federal firearms charges. Stevens and his family denied he was a murderer. "I am not the Green River killer. The Green River Task Force has not treated me or my family fairly," Stevens wrote in a statement in July 1989.

Bob Stevens of Spokane proclaimed his brother was a scapegoat and was being railroaded by the Task Force because they couldn't find the real killer. Bob Stevens and other family members compiled credit-card records, photographs of family vacations and other materials they claimed showed he was someplace else when Green River victims disappeared.

Green River Task Force investigators continued to call Stevens a "viable suspect," but on Nov. 30, 1989, they announced he had been cleared and was no longer under investigation. Stevens remained in federal custody and pleaded guilty to being a felon and a fugitive in possession of a firearm. On Jan. 10, 1990, a judge suspended a 17-month sentence for three years of supervised probation. Stevens died Sept. 30, 1991, of pancreatic cancer, six days before his 41st birthday.

While the probe of Stevens stretched through the summer and fall of 1989, Gary and Judith Ridgway moved from the house in SeaTac to a home on South 253rd Street in Des Moines, a few blocks west of Pacific Highway South.

In 1997, Bob Stevens reversed his position and announced that his brother really was the Green River killer after all. He established a Web site asking people to e-mail tips in the case and he said he was writing a book about his brother and the Green River case. In 2003, when Ridgway confessed to the killings, Bob Stevens said he believed his brother was a member of a group of men responsible for the Green River murders. His Web site was still up and running and a statement by Bob Stevens said he still planned to write the book that would explain everything.

On the 10th anniversary of the Green River killings in 1992, the original Task Force commander, Capt. Frank Adamson, said no one wanted the killer to be found more than he did. But he was realistic: "It is possible there is no solution."

Marcus R. Donner
In 1992 Green River Task Force Detectives Thomas Jensen and James Doyon stand beside file cabinets containing 50,000 pages of tips.

The Missing Decade
Chapter 16

THE PREVAILING THEORY throughout the 1990s was that the Green River killer was either dead, gone or doing time on an unrelated crime. Or maybe the Green River killer was a myth. "It could be two, maybe even three, separate serial murder cases," said Robert Evans, who commanded the Green River Task Force at that time. But the Green River killer did exist, and he was here all along, living in the camouflage of a steady job, loyal wife and a nice home in the Seattle suburbs.

In his 2003 confession, Ridgway described himself as "semi-retired" during the previous decade. He reluctantly admitted to killing twice during the 1990s, but was unimpressed with his work, referring to the murders of Marta Reeves and Patricia Yellowrobe as "amateur."

It was "like I was back starting all over again, and I wasn't a well-greased machine. I was ... I was rusty," the Green River killer told detectives. Pressed to confirm when he killed his last victim, Ridgway at first insisted that he had stopped killing in 1985. As interviews progressed, he changed that to 1987, then 1991, then 1998 and finally to some indefinite time before his arrest in November 2001. In his plea bargain, he accepted blame for just two murders during his final decade as a free man.

Ridgway appeared to live a conventional life during the 1990s. He and his wife, Judith, took RV trips up and down the West Coast. He kept up his yard and tended to his garden. He shared a beer or two with a neighbor on occasion. He often had garage sales at his house in Des Moines, where he lived until 1997. Gary and Judith moved that year to a four-bedroom, 2,300-square-foot house on Auburn's West Hill. Ridgway painted the house a soft yellow color. He was considered a good neighbor and by some, a nice, ordinary guy, at least most of the time.

"They had numerous garage sales," said Beverly Du Fresne, who lived in the cul-de-sac behind the Ridgways in Des Moines. "Some of us thought he should get a business license." Ridgway took garage sales and swap meets seriously. His one brush with the law during the decade was over a swap meet, and it was Ridgway, ice water in his veins, who sought the assistance of police. It was May 12, 1990. Ridgway was selling merchandise at the Midway Swap Meet on Pacific Highway South. He walked away for a few minutes and when he returned a box full of distributor caps and rotors was gone. Ridgway felt wronged and did what any citizen would do. He reported the incident to the Kent Police Department.

Neighbors described Ridgway as soft-spoken, gentle, talkative, hyperactive and sometimes unpredictable. Clem Gregurek, whose rear fence touched a corner of Ridgway's property, got to know Ridgway well enough to cross over to his back yard now and then. Over a beer, they would talk about the weather, gardening and hunting, but nothing too personal. "He was always hyper," Gregurek said. "He walked and worked fast."

Jeff Ross, who lived in the house directly behind Gary and Judith Ridgway until Ridgway's arrest in 2001, recalled having a conversation with Ridgway about how nice it was having a stand of trees between their yards for privacy. Strangely, two weeks later, Ridgway cut down the trees. Ross was stunned and asked Ridgway why he leveled the trees. Ridgway charged at Ross and screamed that he would do whatever he wanted on his own property. Ross turned around and walked away. Another time Ross remembers being awakened early on a Sunday morning by the sound of Ridgway digging in his back yard with a backhoe. This time, Ross didn't ask any questions, although he did later tell investigators about the incident.

As Ridgway walked his Jekyll-and-Hyde tightrope, the Green River Task Force went into hibernation. King County Sheriff Jim Montgomery made the call in 1990 to essentially disband the Task Force. "The fact is, we have to equate our manpower with the amount of information we have to work with at the time," Montgomery said. An impressive assemblage of law enforcement agents that at its peak in the mid-1980s included as many as 60 detectives became a dormant two-detective team — Thomas Jensen and James Doyon. In the summer of 2000, it was cut to just Jensen.

Jensen spent most of his time alone, tediously calling up lists of names and bytes of evidence on his computer screen, seeking correlations. The telephone would ring at least once each day. The tips were usually bogus, and the caller on the other end of the line was usually someone obsessed with the case. Still, Jensen listened to all of them, because it would take just one good tip to catch the killer. Even Ridgway called in once in the mid-1990s. He reported finding a bloody sheet near his house. "We thought that was really interesting," Jensen said. The blood was tested and turned out to be the blood of a deer. Jensen figured Ridgway was "just chuckling under his breath."

Detective Dave Reichert also stepped aside in 1990 after being promoted to sergeant. It had been eight frustrating years for the future sheriff, whose pursuit of the Green River killer had become an obsession. Still, Reichert mustered some optimism as he left his work to be carried out by others. "I just have to believe that the guy's name is in our files," Reichert said in April 1990. "I couldn't have done this for eight years if I didn't think this case would be solved."

There were no more killing rampages like the one that occurred between 1982 and 1984. In the 1990s, Ridgway became a more mature murderer with increased self-control. Most people thought the killings were over. As serial killer Ted Bundy said of the Green River killer in the hours before Bundy's 1989 execution: "He's either moved, he's dead, or he's doing something very different."

Ridgway was never able to shake his appetite for murder, but he was able to subdue it for extended periods. Still, he was drawn to the Strip, Ridgway's lifelong home away from home. Ridgway continued to seek out prostitutes, who by this point had been hit hard by the crack epidemic. Ridgway once remarked to detectives that the crack-addicted prostitutes were great because they charged less.

Still, the Strip was changing, becoming less a haven for streetwalkers. Ironically, Ridgway was at least partly responsible for the noticeable improvements. The area near the airport incorporated, becoming the city of SeaTac in February 1990, in part to renew its image. The first order of business: Clean up the Strip. Pacific Highway South was renamed International Boulevard. The new city's leaders immediately adopted a Stay Out of Areas of Prostitution ordinance and implemented enhanced penalties for soliciting prostitution.

The reformation was largely successful, and in most people's minds the Green River killer receded into historical legend. Investigators talked openly about the frustrating nature of this case and began considering it could wind up as much a mystery as the identity of Jack the Ripper or San Francisco's Zodiac killer. Detectives who had painstakingly worked the Green River case for a decade still considered Ridgway a top suspect, but there was no suspicion that he was still killing. Co-workers at Kenworth knew of Ridgway's appetite for streetwalkers and brushes with the law, but few of them considered him a serious threat.

Others noticed odd behavior that always made them wonder.

"We called him Green River Gary or G.R.," said Bob Schweiss, a cab builder at Kenworth who worked with Ridgway for nine years. "A lot of us thought he was just goofy enough to be the guy."

Cheryl Ardt worked with Ridgway from 1990 until his arrest.

"He was very, very weird," she said. "He would get up in your face and ask you where did you live." Ardt recalled Ridgway's locker being full of trash he picked up at work, such as paper towels people had used to wipe their hands. In the lunch room, the truck painter was too friendly, trying too hard. But he was never angry or threatening. He often could be found reading his Bible and was open about his relationship with God, Schweiss said. "I'd be curious to know if he was seeking some kind of forgiveness."

FBI profilers said the man who went on a killing spree in the early 1980s could not simply stop killing. Bundy agreed during a death-row interview with Green River detectives: "Not unless he was born again and got filled with the Holy Spirit in a very real way," Bundy said. The interviews with Bundy were recounted in "The Riverman: Ted Bundy and I Hunt for the Green River Killer" by Bob Keppel, the chief consultant to the Green River Task Force. The book was the second on the Green River killer. The first, "The Search for the Green River Killer," by Carlton Smith and Tomas Guillen, was published in 1991. A third book related to the killer came out in 2002: "Through a Mother's Eyes," by Kathy Mills, the mother of Opal Mills, the fifth victim of the Green River killer.

Although Ridgway was able to curb his appetite for killing, the same could not be said for his obsession with prostitutes. In an interview with detectives in 1987, Ridgway compared his attraction to prostitutes to a drug addiction. "It's a compulsion," Ridgway said. "They affect me like alcohol does an alcoholic."

And Ridgway would fall off the wagon at least twice in the 1990s. He would later say he was able to stop for months at a time, something that can only be considered an achievement when compared with the early 1980s, when he once tried to kill two prostitutes in one day. Before Ridgway's arrest, detectives did not link the Green River killer to any murders during the 1990s, despite several bodies of women and girls found in wooded areas of King County during the decade.

The body of 36-year-old Marta Reeves, who got hooked on cocaine and began prostituting herself in 1989, was found east of Enumclaw on Sept. 20, 1990. She had been killed earlier the same year. Police said at the time that it was "very unlikely" that Reeves was a victim of the Green River killer. Thirteen years later, Ridgway admitted to killing Reeves. In his plea negotiations he also accepted responsibility for the murder of Patricia Ann Yellowrobe, a 38-year-old woman found dead in 1998. Yellowrobe's death had previously been listed as a drug overdose.

Ridgway would later say he could not recall the details of what led up to the murder of Reeves, the mother of four children. When reminded he had left her driver's license in a mailbox, he said he did that on occasion. Asked why, Ridgway said: "I don't know. Get back at the family or something."

In the case of Yellowrobe's 1998 murder, which Ridgway called an "aberration," he allowed his victim to dress after they had sex. Maybe Ridgway had not planned to kill Yellowrobe, but he became enraged, he said, because he wasn't satisfied with Yellowrobe's performance. "I just didn't wanna pay for somebody just layin' around," Ridgway told detectives.

The Green River killer continued to kill until at least 1998. Why many of the bodies found during the decade weren't considered the killer's victims will remain a topic of conversation. Detective Jensen always believed the list of 49 victims was too short. He estimated the actual death toll in the mid-50s or higher. Jensen said departmental politics got in the way of giving proper consideration to the possibility that bodies turning up in the 1990s could be Green River victims.

Agency politics may have hindered the investigation, but politics had no impact on the extraordinary scientific advances that were taking place during the mid-1990s. Throughout the decade, Jensen and the Task Force possessed the link between Ridgway and victims of the Green River killer, collected from the victims when the first bodies were found.

A developing DNA technology was nipping at the heels of Ridgway and hundreds of other murderers and rapists who left a microscopic DNA imprint of themselves with their victims. The new technology, polymerase chain reaction-short tandem repeats, or PCR-STR, would provide what two decades of police work could not: An irrefutable link between Gary Leon Ridgway and three victims of the Green River killer.

Matt Brashears
Biological evidence from the investigation of Gary Ridgway sits frozen at 25 degrees at Task Force headquarters.

The Break
Chapter 17

SHERIFF DAVE REICHERT REMEMBERS one day in early September 2001 as perhaps the happiest in his long career as a cop. Detective Tom Jensen, who for most of a decade had kept the Green River case alive, had unbelievable news, and had been waiting for days to share it.

In March, hoping to take advantage of advances in DNA typing, Jensen asked the Washington State Patrol Crime Lab to analyze several DNA samples from the case. Jensen got confirmation of the results on Sept. 4 or 5 at the crime lab in downtown Seattle. They had a match. He walked across the street to the County Courthouse to tell Reichert the news. But the sheriff was on vacation and wouldn't be back for a week. So Jensen and a handful of others very close to the investigation sat on the big news. A week passed and a new meeting was set for 3:30 p.m. Sept. 10. Jensen and the others were kept waiting for 45 minutes when a staff meeting ran late. "I bawled him out for that," Jensen said.

Jensen had three charts to show Reichert that would help explain, in a simple way, the complexities of DNA profiling. For the first time a physical connection was revealed between two of the early victims found in or near the Green River — Marcia Chapman and Opal Mills — and a longtime suspect. The lab also was working on a DNA profile that would link the same suspect to Carol Christensen.

A pivotal third chart connected Chapman and Mills to the suspect, based on semen found on their bodies. "This was the DNA profile of the Green River killer," Jensen told Reichert. Who is it? Reichert asked. With tears in his eyes, Jensen handed the sheriff an envelope. Inside was a photograph. Reichert held the envelope to his head.

"I don't even have to open it," Reichert told Jensen. "It's Gary Ridgway."

The Kenworth truck painter who killed at least 48 young women, the man who co-workers nicknamed Green River Gary, had been in the area all along. Ridgway had managed to escape detection despite several close calls, despite being interviewed numerous times as a suspect, despite being accused by a victim's father, despite taking a lie-detector test, despite having his car and home searched and the results examined by forensic scientists, despite never leaving the area and despite spending nearly two decades near the top of the list of possible Green River suspects.

Reichert had long believed Ridgway was *the* suspect in the Green River killings. Now, for the first time, he had almost irrefutable evidence — DNA, the building blocks of life. The testing directly connected Ridgway to at least three of the 49 victims on the Task Force list. Ridgway was almost certainly the Green River killer, but it would take more evidence to convict him in court. Ridgway could simply claim he had sex with those three, but was not their killer.

In great secrecy, Reichert went about getting that evidence. Sgt. D.B. Gates suggested that Reichert form an evidence review team that would operate under the radar to start building the case against Ridgway. The next day, a fateful day in the nation's history — Sept. 11, 2001 — Reichert asked Jim Graddon to head up the team. Graddon had patrolled the SeaTac Strip during the heyday of prostitution in the 1980s and may have arrested one of the Green River victims. On Sept. 13, Graddon was one of the few told about the DNA results, and he kept it — and his new job — quiet. "In 25 years, it was probably the best-kept secret in law enforcement," Graddon said. "That was critical to us."

Graddon and the others assigned to the team were lucky they still had evidence to sift through. Years earlier some of the top brass in the Sheriff's Office thought it was time to clean house and throw out the boxes of evidence stored at a secure warehouse in south Seattle. But Reichert and other detectives fought against it. They prevailed. Cops don't like loose ends.

Safe in a freezer in that Seattle warehouse were DNA samples taken from Ridgway in 1987 and the contents of rape kits collected after the bodies of Opal Mills, Carol Christensen and Marcia Chapman were recovered. In 1988, a forensics lab in New York tried to conduct a DNA test, but the samples were too small for technology available at the time to develop a profile. The lab had Ridgway's sample, too, but without something to compare it to, a profile wasn't done.

During a routine review of the evidence in 1997, Jensen came across the gauze that Ridgway chewed on in 1987. Jensen submitted the "gauze chew" to the state crime lab for DNA profiling in November. Despite the deteriorated state of the sample, a profile was made — the first ever of Ridgway's DNA. The wait would continue, until scientists at the state lab were able to apply a more sensitive DNA typing technique to link Ridgway in somewhat uncertain terms to Mills and Chapman, and conclusively to Christensen.

In early September, Dr. Beverly Himick, a forensic scientist with the crime lab, called Jensen with the initial results. "She is the one who caught the Green River killer. Let's face it," Jensen said.

But it was the science that caught the killer, Himick said. She spent much of the summer trying to coax enough genetic material from the swabs collected on the rape kits to do a DNA profile. The task was even harder because scientists in the 1980s trying to do their own profile destroyed part of the gauze and in some cases, only the stick was left. In the case of Opal Mills, Himick didn't even have that. But detectives had preserved some of Opal's pubic hairs. Using a special rinse, Himick found sperm from Gary Ridgway hanging from one. Unfortunately for Ridgway, he had left Opal's body on the bank of the Green River. If he had dumped her in the river like Chapman and

Cynthia Hinds, the evidence might have been washed away.

The highly sophisticated tests also cleared two other suspects in the case — Melvyn Foster and John Norris Hanks, who in early 1983 had passed a lie-detector test. Foster, now, was really in the clear, two decades after he called to help police find the killer and instead became a suspect.

Detectives still weren't ready to move on Ridgway. They wanted to develop more evidence. But they watched him. On Oct. 17, 2001, detectives followed as Ridgway took the least-direct route from his job in Renton to his home on Auburn's West Hill. Instead of a quick trip on Interstate 5, he drove down Pacific Highway South from SeaTac to Auburn, driving below the speed limit and for a time distracted by a woman on the street who appeared to be a prostitute. Ridgway followed much the same routine on Oct. 23, making two U-turns on Pacific Highway. On his way home, he stopped at the home in McMicken Heights where his mother had lived until she died two months earlier. After her death, Ridgway and his brothers put the house up for sale.

The surveillance ended, but detectives were still busy preparing, reviewing and developing evidence. Ridgway was busy, too. On Friday, Nov. 16, when Ridgway was not under surveillance, he prowled Pacific Highway South in his red Ford Ranger pickup truck. He spotted a prostitute walking near the Motel 6. He waved cash at her through the truck's window, then pulled his truck into a parking lot. He wanted to know if she was "dating." She was interested, but Ridgway thought a cop was watching from the cemetery lot up the street. She agreed to meet him down the road. Instead, she signaled her partner. She was an undercover cop. Ridgway was arrested carrying $30 and latex gloves. (In court on Nov. 27, he was fined $700 and told to stay away from prostitutes.)

As he was interviewed during booking at the King County Jail in Seattle, Ridgway asked police not to call his wife to verify his identity. Instead, he suggested, "You can contact the Green River Task Force. They know me real well." That didn't happen. Only by coincidence, 11 days later, did detectives in the small circle who knew that Ridgway had been identified as the Green River killer learn of his arrest. Just after Thanksgiving, a detective doing some routine investigative work on his computer came across Ridgway's arrest. It was now clear that Ridgway was still on patrol, and detectives moved quickly.

Surveillance resumed. On Nov. 28, 2001, Gary Ridgway was down to his last two days as a free man. It was a Wednesday — a work day — and Ridgway got up very early. He left the house at 4:20 a.m., and for the next hour, detectives followed. From Ridgway's home in Auburn, it was a 20-minute drive to the Kenworth plant in Renton. The quickest route was the freeway, either Interstate 5 or State Route 167, but Ridgway went another way. He cut over to Pacific Highway South, and a drive that should have taken 20 minutes lasted an hour. He drove slowly, lingering at intersections, watching for movement. In the chill, morning darkness, no one stirred, and Ridgway finally gave up the hunt.

When he pulled his Ford pickup into the Kenworth parking lot, it was just 5:20 a.m., and Ridgway was 45 minutes early for his shift.

His prostitution arrest left those who knew about the DNA results with unsettling questions. For the past decade, there had been no murders linked to the Green River killer, and experts who study serial murders had begun to speculate that the killer was gone. Maybe he was in jail. Maybe he was dead. Maybe he was killing somewhere else. Now it appeared that the experts were wrong. Gary Ridgway was almost certainly the Green River killer, and he had been here all along. Not only was he alive, he was still pursuing his obsessions.

But he would never kill again. Two days later, Gary Ridgway would go to jail forever.

Matt Brashears
Green River killer Gary Ridgway is led into the courtroom April 15, 2002, when prosecutors announced they would seek the death penalty.

The Arrest
Chapter 18

NOV. 30, 2001. SHERIFF DAVE REICHERT paced back and forth at homicide headquarters inside the Regional Justice Center in Kent. He was surrounded by several detectives who had worked the Green River case in the 1980s. "We were all on pins and needles," Reichert said of the anxious moments before Ridgway's arrest. Meanwhile at Kenworth Truck Co. in Renton, a few miles to the north, Ridgway was painting his last truck. At 3 p.m., Ridgway's shift ended, as did his life as a free man.

The call came over the police radio: "We have one in custody." Ridgway was apprehended without incident. Homicide HQ went quiet for a moment. The silence turned to an emotional cheer followed by hugs and tears; countless tears of sorrow and frustration were now tears of joy.

It was two veterans of the Green River investigation, detectives Jim Doyon and Randy Mullinax, who arrested Ridgway outside the Kenworth plant. The detectives drove Ridgway to the Regional Justice Center in Kent, read him his rights and then launched into an explanation of why he was under arrest. "I think I should probably have a lawyer," Ridgway responded. The detectives handed the suspected killer a phone book. By now, lawyers were already beginning to contact the Sheriff's Office after hearing of the arrest on television and radio. Ridgway thumbed through the phone book. "After 20 minutes of running his finger down the page, I asked him if he had found anyone," said veteran detective Tom Jensen. Ridgway said, "I don't know who to call."

Ridgway would later tell his attorneys he didn't know what had triggered his arrest. Did police know that he had fallen "off the wagon and killed" just three years earlier? Had they linked him to the 1998 killing of Patricia Yellowrobe, whose body he had dumped in a gravel parking lot of a tow yard in South Park? Or was this the beginning of another of those intense periods of scrutiny, where police questioned and searched, then went away, because they still had no proof?

Ridgway was then assigned a public defender from the Associated Council for the Accused. Greg Girard, who supervises felony cases for the agency, headed for the justice center, calling another public defender, Mark Prothero, on the way. Prothero was poolside, coaching the Kentwood High School boys swim team, when a parent walked by and told Prothero of Ridgway's arrest. After swim practice, Prothero went to his Kent office, picked up Girard's message and headed for the justice center. Girard and Prothero talked with Ridgway for about an hour, explaining what would happen next and questioning him closely about what he had told detectives. At about 8 p.m. Prothero left phone messages with Ridgway's wife, Judith, and his older brother, Gregory, telling them that Ridgway was OK and that he had someone on his side. At that point, Prothero said, Ridgway was "relatively calm." Later, veteran defense attorney Anthony Savage and others joined Ridgway's defense team.

Ridgway would eventually be transferred to the ultra-security unit of the King County Jail. He would be held there for investigation of four counts of aggravated first-degree murder in the deaths of Marcia Faye Chapman, Cynthia Hinds, Opal Charmaine Mills and Carol Ann Christensen.

After the brief celebration, Reichert immediately got on the phone and started calling others who had been involved with the case to tell them the news. The sheriff didn't want them to hear about it on television. Garrett Mills, the older brother of Green River killer victim Opal Mills, was overcome by a flood of emotions. "It's 20 years now, but as soon as they start showing her picture, it's like it just happened again," Mills said. "I remember Reichert coming to our house. He had black hair then. Now he has gray hair."

Less than two hours after the arrest, local reporters and photographers converged on the sheriff's headquarters in downtown Seattle and crammed into Reichert's office for a press conference. Mug shots of the mustachioed Gary Leon Ridgway were passed out to the media, who would broadcast his face on television reports and on the front pages of the next day's papers. For a moment, this was the biggest story in the world. One of the longest, most expensive manhunts in American history was over.

Reichert was clearly emotional as he sat behind his desk, microphones in his face and cameras clicking as he spoke. Gary Leon Ridgway has been arrested today for the deaths of four of the victims on the list of Green River homicides, said the sheriff, stopping well short of the sound bite reporters coveted. "Sheriff, you haven't said this guy is the Green River killer. Is this the Green River killer?" a reporter asked. Reichert's words were measured. He didn't want to jump the gun or jeopardize his case against Ridgway. "I cannot say with certainty that Gary Ridgway is responsible for all of those deaths ... but boy, have we made one giant step forward."

Ridgway had long been considered a prime suspect in the murders. "I always felt that Gary Ridgway was one of the top five suspects," the sheriff said. "There was always a top five, and Gary Ridgway was always one of those, right up in front."

It was forensic science that finally caught up to Ridgway, but Reichert made a point of telling reporters that without smart and dedicated police work, there would have been no DNA evidence to analyze.

While the sheriff primarily spoke of profound joy for the families of the victims and complete vindication for himself and his department, he exhibited a tinge of bitterness toward the media over some critical and sometimes cruel portrayals of the Green River Task Force in the 1980s. It had been two decades, but Reichert was still stinging from some of the shots taken at the Task Force. Several of the reporters present were in elementary school and junior high when the Green River murders began.

For investigators, there was much more work to do. "We want to make sure he's responsible for all those murders," Reichert said.

As word leaked of Ridgway's arrest, reporters bolted for Auburn to get reaction from Ridgway's wife, Judith, and neighbors. The press arrived before police were able to turn Ridgway's home into a crime scene. Several reporters knocked on the front door, but Mrs. Ridgway declined to comment.

Within hours, detectives were digging up the lawns at Ridgway's current and former homes, ripping out the carpets and searching inside the walls, looking for any shred of evidence that would link him to more murders. At a house in Des Moines that was Gary and Judith Ridgway's home in 1992, detectives and deputies kicked rocks aside and tipped flower pots in a small garden beneath a gently swaying flag mounted on the front porch. Christmas lights were strung along a chain-link fence in front of the white house, but it was crime-scene spotlights and patrol car headlights that illuminated the home. Yellow police tape outlined the quarter-acre property.

The defense team's strategy would be to raise a reasonable doubt by investigating the hundreds of men who had been considered possible suspects over the years — and to somehow spare Ridgway's life. Meanwhile, King County Prosecutor Norm Maleng declared the county would seek the death penalty should Ridgway be found guilty. And one thing was becoming abundantly clear: Cash-strapped King County was headed for the most expensive trial in its history. The taxpayers of King County were faced with the prospect of forking over untold millions not only to prosecute the suspected Green River killer — but to defend him, as well.

Matt Brashears
King County Sheriff's Office spokesman Sgt. John Urquhart with a wall of boxed evidence at a secure warehouse in south Seattle.

The Case
Chapter 19

GARY RIDGWAY'S HOME for the next 18 and a half months was a small cell in the King County Jail in downtown Seattle, where he would have plenty of time to think about what he had done and what he would say about it.

Deemed a high-security inmate, he would sit in an 8x10-foot cell for 23 hours per day, his meals shoved through a small slot in the door. He was allowed visitors, and his brothers and at first his wife, Judith, came to see him regularly. He was moved on occasion to similar cells in the jail, standard procedure for ultra-security inmates. He was allowed an hour per day in a day room about twice the size of his cell, where he could exercise. He spent his time in there alone as well. He could read — books, magazines and newspapers — and shower, but there was no television. He was allowed unlimited collect phone calls, and he often called family members — his wife, two brothers and adult son.

The next year and a half became a series of meetings with attorneys. Monthly court hearings would be his only outings from the jail, feet chained together, hands cuffed and shackled to his waist.

Ridgway tried to pay his lead lawyer, famed defense attorney Anthony Savage, to defend him against the charges. County taxpayers footed the rest of the bill for what ultimately became a defense team of about two dozen people, the size of a small law firm. The team included seven full-time attorneys, plus two more who shared an eighth attorney position. There were also seven investigators and positions for eight paralegals, although more than that worked in the slots, some part-time.

Dan Satterberg, chief of staff of the King County Prosecutor's Office, likened the team to "not just a Porsche, but an entire Porsche dealership." The press leaped upon the comment like children on Christmas presents.

The cost of the case would reach millions in the next year and a half — for the continuing investigation by police and prosecutors, the defense investigation of their client and his case — while county parks and pools closed, and taxpayers began to complain bitterly. The closings weren't the result of the costs of the case. All of King County was cutting back to make up for a budget shortfall, but the public connected the two. When King County Councilman Pete von Reichbauer ran an online poll asking if too much money was being spent on the Ridgway case, 93 percent of those who answered the question said yes.

It wouldn't be the most expensive case in the country. The trial of Oklahoma City bomber Tim McVeigh, involving 168 victims, cost tens of millions. But with the national average of a capital case being around $2 million, Ridgway's case — which hit the $12.7 million mark before the plea deal was filed — was clearly far from the norm. Counties across the United States have strapped themselves to pay for such cases and sometimes have nearly gone bankrupt.

These costs came on top of an estimated $15 million that had been spent over the years for the Green River investigation.

Judge Richard Jones, a King County Superior Court judge for eight years, was selected to preside over what would be the most expensive criminal case in the state's history. The former King County prosecutor and assistant U.S. attorney for the Western

District of Washington had lectured at legal education programs for the state and county bar associations, state trial lawyer's association and the University of Washington. He is also the brother of music producer Quincy Jones. The defense had asked for a preassigned judge, someone who would handle the entire case. Criminal cases in King County Superior Court are normally assigned to the next available judge, and often just before trial is set to begin. But the request had been made by defense attorneys, and prosecutors, in cases before. Preassignment benefits both sides, providing consistency in rulings based on the judge's familiarity with the complexities of a case.

A no-nonsense man, Jones presided over monthly status conferences and other hearings. When the attorneys were unable to reach agreements over items of evidence or whether depositions could be taken, Jones made decisions quickly. He began each hearing by telling the parties what documents he had received since the previous hearing and then asking if he had everything he should have. He then went through motions and requests in the order received, giving attorneys on both sides enough time to argue their points, sometimes repeatedly. The hearings were methodical, but they moved along at a brisk pace, and it was clear who was in charge.

As county budget hearings got under way, and County Council members questioned the cost of the Ridgway trial, Jones also had stern warnings for them regarding Ridgway's right to a fair trial. At one point, Jones ordered the council to take action on a $1.9 million request from the defense that would allow Ridgway's attorneys to continue their work.

At the request of the Office of Public Defense, Jones appointed a special master to review the defense requests for funding. Special masters aren't normally used in criminal cases, but rather as mediators in civil lawsuits and in some family courts across the country. Many said at the time they couldn't recall a special master being used before in a criminal case in the state.

If Jones hadn't initially decided to keep the special master's identity from the media, and thereby the public, the decision would likely have been more welcomed. But he decided the special master needed to be protected from political pressure and from those who got angry enough to make threats. That brought even more criticism — millions of dollars of tax money were to be reviewed in secrecy by an unknown person. Some of the resentment was directed toward defense attorneys. Mark Prothero and Todd Gruenhagen got threatening letters and calls.

After repeated media requests and public complaints, Jones identified the special master as Kate Pflaumer, former U.S. attorney for Western Washington. One reason for the earlier secrecy was concern after the Oct. 11, 2001, slaying of her former colleague, assistant U.S. attorney and community activist Tom Wales. He had been gunned down while working at his computer in his Queen Anne home. The killing, which police called an execution-style hit, remains unsolved. There were rumors that Pflaumer might quit the case over security concerns, but she stayed on.

•••

Lead defense attorneys Savage and Prothero focused on different aspects of the case. Savage assumed Ridgway was innocent and he and Gruenhagen jumped into trial preparation, as did Michele Shaw, Eric Lindell, Fred Leatherman and Dave Roberson. Shaw also acted as a liaison with Ridgway's family members. Gruenhagen focused on the non-DNA forensic aspects, and Prothero and Leatherman focused on the DNA.

Prothero also took charge of the penalty phase, which would come if Ridgway was convicted. That required him to operate from the premise that his client would be found guilty. Prothero would later say that he always doubted Ridgway was completely innocent. "It's just the safest way to act in any aggravated murder case. Always prepare for the worst and hope for the best," Prothero said at the time.

In the penalty phase of a capital trial, the defense presents evidence that the defendant deserves to live, while prosecutors tell the jury why the defendant deserves to die. It's a mini-trial, with each side trying to prove its case. The same jury that decides guilt later decides whether the defendant is sentenced to death.

A highly recommended mitigation expert, Mary Goody, of Jackson, Wyo., was retained to look deeply into every aspect of Ridgway's life. Goody has repeatedly said she couldn't comment about the case.

Mitigation specialists spend months researching a defendant's background. They interview family members, friends, employees, employers, co-workers and neighbors. They also review medical and psychological/psychiatric records, and provide workups of family and work histories. "They basically investigate from birth to the time of the incident for which they're charged. You need to have a context for the person who's accused of these crimes," explained defense attorney Al Kitching, who has worked several capital cases in his 25-year career in Seattle. "They aren't born bad. They don't start out at age 1 saying, 'When I'm 25, I'm going to go and commit this crime.'

"You try to find the things that make the person human," he added. "Many are accused of awful things that seem inhuman, make them seem like they're just cold-blooded killers, but very often there's a whole other side to them."

In Washington, prosecutors decide whether to ask for the death penalty in an aggravated murder case after they receive what is called a mitigation packet. It is submitted in various forms, including printed material and audio and video tapes. Sometimes, defense attorneys make personal presentations using their materials. Under Washington state law, mitigating factors include such things as mental illness, abuse or neglect as a child and lack of criminal history. Such factors are often used not only before the death penalty decision is made, but also in the penalty phase of the trial.

The mitigation information isn't made public, unless defense attorneys want to discuss it. And they haven't.

Ridgway was told by his attorneys that they could mount a defense despite the DNA evidence against him. But they also warned him that if another forensic link appeared, they would have to re-evaluate the case to decide how to handle it. He had told Savage in the first week after his arrest that he wasn't guilty, but they didn't discuss his "innocence" in detail.

•••

Ridgway declined to appear at his Dec. 1, 2001, bail hearing. His no-show disappointed a lone friend of a Green River victim, and also the more than 30 reporters and photographers from all over the country who had come to see one of the most elusive serial killers ever. Those same journalists were even more dejected when the sound was turned off just before Ridgway's hearing began and King County Court Commissioner Anne Harper could not turn it back on. Cameras and bright television lights were everywhere as people stood on benches and walked over each other, trying to get the best vantage point.

Senior Deputy Prosecutor Jeff Baird declined to answer questions as he left. It would become his pattern — and those of prosecutors Patricia Eakes, Brian McDonald, Ian Goodhew and Sean O'Donnell — throughout the next 18 months. They said they did not want to try the case in the media.

Meanwhile, deputies searched every house Ridgway had lived in, moving current residents of the homes into motel rooms and telling them they would be compensated for any damage done to their homes. Displacing the current residents of the homes was unusual. John Urquhart, a 25-year veteran of the sheriff's department and its spokesman, said he had never seen such a thing done. But this was an exceptional case, and now that they had him in custody, Sheriff Dave Reichert vowed to make it so tight that Ridgway would either be convicted and put to death or forced to tell everything about the victims he had killed.

Carpets were torn out, paint was scraped, everything in each home was examined thoroughly. Officials in white spacelike jumpsuits, shoe coverings and surgical-style masks were seen coming and going from the houses. Neighbors were questioned by police and the media, and most said they were shocked by Ridgway's arrest because he had always been quiet and nice. A backhoe and cadaver dogs, trained to sniff out human remains, were brought in to search the grounds of his home in Auburn. They also searched his former home in SeaTac, where investigators would later learn that many of the killings had been committed.

Ridgway's Dec. 18 arraignment was less of a media event than the earlier bail hearing, but security was tight — so tight that Prothero couldn't get into the glass-enclosed part of the courtroom after the hearing had started. Family members and friends of victims came, representing many more victims than the four with which Ridgway was then charged. They said they were certain that he was the killer, and they needed to see him in person.

Savage told the journalists who clustered around him after the arraignment that Ridgway was innocent, that his wife was standing behind him, and that he had thought his days as a Green River suspect were over after the 1987 search of his home and person.

"He seems like an innocent man who's in a lot of trouble," Savage said.

• • •

Court documents came in a flood in the following months. Details police had learned over the years but had sealed were opened to the public. Those following the case learned of Ridgway's appetite for sex and of an incident when he choked his second wife from police interviews with wives and girlfriends that had been conducted years earlier.

Meanwhile, family members and friends of the victims talked with the media, trying to relieve the pain of reopened wounds that had never really healed.

And although prosecutors said it would be months before a decision would be made on whether the death penalty would be sought in the case, Savage told the media that a request for Ridgway's death would come "as sure as tomorrow's sunrise."

Investigators who had been on the Task Force a decade or two earlier attended the initial hearings. Some said they believed all along that Ridgway was the killer. Others said they believed some of the killings may have been committed by copycats.

• • •

King County Prosecutor Norm Maleng initially took a hard line. He would not bargain with the death penalty, he said sternly in his first news conference after the arrest — not even if it meant the families of seven women whose bodies had never been found would go without finding out what happened to their loved ones.

"Besides, a lot of people who kill a lot of people would then have a bargaining chip, where someone who killed one or two people would not," he added.

As the court case moved through its first year, the bills piled up and so did the work. Defense attorneys insisted Ridgway couldn't get a fair trial in the Seattle area, and there was talk of having the trial in Portland. Another suggestion was to bring jurors in from other counties for the trial.

The defense attorneys begged the media to lower its spotlight on the case, and the glare did indeed lessen. Fewer and fewer reporters attended what would become monthly status conferences to keep up on the case, until only two or three, often newspaper rather than television reporters, showed up each month.

The defense had a lot of catching up to do. They were told that more than a million documents existed and that police had checked out more than 500 suspects in the case. The attorneys knew they would have to do the same; anything they could use to implicate someone else in even one killing might be the reasonable doubt they would need to prevent a conviction.

In the meantime, investigators buckled down, reviewing evidence they had collected over nearly 20 years to see if they could connect Ridgway to more than four killings. Reichert turned down book, movie and television show offers, saying that he didn't want anyone to profit from the case that he readily admitted had consumed a good portion of his life.

The Task Force was reformed and its headquarters moved to a county-owned building at Boeing Field. Fourteen detectives were assigned to the case and had individual cubicles in the building. For the first time, it was more than enough space. A large poster of victim photos was hung inside the building.

Between 8,000 and 10,000 pieces of evidence had been collected, and investigators began going through them; prosecutors sent hundreds of items to the Washington State Patrol Crime Lab and public and private labs around the country to see if Ridgway could be linked to other slayings. Just the task of finding Ridgway's vehicles was huge; police said he had possibly had access to 100 of them over the years, including vehicles he could have borrowed from family members and vehicles he worked on for other people. Police purchased several vehicles from outside the state and brought them to Seattle. They scoured them for trace evidence, such as blood or other body fluids, hairs or fibers.

The mother of victim Opal Mills filed a wrongful death lawsuit against Ridgway in civil court and wrote a book about her daughter. One of the last places the girl had been seen was at church. Her family ached for the troubled girl, whom they insisted was not a prostitute.

Serial murder expert Robert Keppel's book, "The Riverman," was reissued, with Ridgway's face on the cover instead of serial killer Ted Bundy's. Neither Keppel, who had worked on both cases, nor Savage was happy to have such a thing occur before a conviction. Ridgway's name and face, and Reichert's, turned up in magazines and newspapers all over the country, and many implied or stated as fact that Ridgway was the Green River killer.

•••

On April 15, 2002, prosecutors announced they would seek the death penalty if Ridgway were convicted of the killings. No one was surprised. Savage said Maleng had painted himself into a corner at his press conference after Ridgway's arrest.

Paige Miley, a career prostitute, and one of the few people who could link Ridgway to the disappearance of a Green River victim, was brought to Seattle from Las Vegas for a deposition. But that was scuttled less than an hour before it was to begin. Prosecutors were ready to proceed, but the defense attorneys argued that they had not been given all the information they needed and therefore did not have enough time to prepare.

A three-hour status conference that morning — May 24, 2002 — began with a summary of what prosecutors had given to the defense but descended into insinuations and sniping by attorneys on both sides. One prosecutor called a defense motion "a paltry pleading." Savage asked for an additional 45 days to prepare for the deposition and Eakes responded that the case wouldn't get to trial until 2011 if it took that much time to prepare for each witness interview.

In July 2002, prosecutors notified the defense of evidence from the cases of three dead and two missing Green River victims they wanted to include in Ridgway's trial, saying they could be linked to him and he was likely responsible for their deaths or disappearances. They stopped short of filing charges in those cases, which would have meant proving the cases beyond a reasonable doubt. Instead, they sought to have them admitted as evidence under court rules that allow "other bad or uncharged acts." Such evidence can be allowed as evidence to prove such things as motive, opportunity, intent, preparation, plan, knowledge or identity.

Their house already on the market, the Ridgways legally separated in September 2002, effectively ending a 14-year marriage. The paperwork had been drawn up months earlier. There was no explanation for the delay between the couple signing the forms and Ridgway having his attorneys file them.

• • •

Also in September 2002, DNA experts failed to identify a bone chip found in Ridgway's SeaTac home during the 1987 search as either human or animal. Technicians found it was too small and too degraded for DNA typing. The testing, called mitochondrial DNA analysis, or mtDNA, was used to identify victims of the World Trade Center attack and has been used to identify remains of MIAs returned from Vietnam. The bone, which weighed approximately 1/40th of an ounce, was destroyed by the testing process.

At the September 2002 status conference, prosecutors asked for the trial to be set for March 16, 2004. At that same hearing, the defense told Judge Jones that they had received more than 400,000 documents related to the case, 40,000 documents from the FBI, 100 DVDs of videotaped witness and suspect statements, hundreds of audiotapes that included witness statements, thousands of photographs and the entire case files of all 49 women believed to be Green River victims. Printing the document would require nearly 840 reams of paper. And although a document database was set up that both prosecutors and defense attorneys could access, it didn't produce reliable search results, the defense repeatedly argued in court.

In early 2003, the Task Force began putting photos of missing women on a Web site and asked the public to help identify them. The women, police said, might have some knowledge of the case or the killer. A March 28, 2003, date was set for prosecutors to announce whether they planned to file additional charges against Ridgway. Hair found at various Green River crime scenes was sent off for mtDNA testing. Hundreds of items of evidence were already being tested across the country. Few people expected that those results would break the case wide open.

On March 27, prosecutors announced they were filing three more murder charges against Ridgway, including one for Wendy Coffield, believed to be the first Green River victim. That brought the total number of charges to seven, including five victims who were found along the Green River in Kent within a 30-day period in the summer of 1982.

As Ridgway sat in court reading the new documents, his expression never changed. And Savage, who was taken by surprise, remained cool under pressure as well. "What they think they can prove and what they can prove are two different things," Savage said just moments later. "Seeing as Gary didn't do it, someone else did." But what the documents contained was stunning to the defense.

The new forensic evidence — paint linking Ridgway to more Green River slayings — was just what defense attorneys had warned him about. "If more evidence comes up that links you with any of these victims, you're done," Ridgway was told. He was cornered.

A detective with the Task Force photographs a bone fragment Aug. 23, 2003, in a wooded area off the Kent/Des Moines Road.

Patrick Hagerty

The Deal
Chapter 20

Part I: Confession

FRIDAY, APRIL 11, 2003.

That was the day Gary Ridgway first admitted that he was the Green River killer. For at least the past two days, he had been thinking about confessing to his attorneys. They said it might buy his life. His family members — including his adult son, wife, his two brothers and their wives — wanted him to live. When Michele Shaw told him, on April 9, Ridgway broke down and cried. On that day, Ridgway admitted to his attorneys that he had some interest in a possible deal, but he hadn't yet come clean, and there would be lies along the way.

On April 10, he took responsibility for about 25 of the 49 victims on the Green River list. But it was on April 11 that he admitted what many of those who knew him would have a hard time believing. He had killed many more women.

His family just couldn't picture Gary Ridgway as the Green River killer. His siblings and son, his co-workers and friends, couldn't fathom that he might have strangled nearly 50 women to death, most of them with his bare hands.

His attorneys had adamantly declared his innocence, although at least initially, some had their doubts. "I guess my gut feeling was that he was responsible for some, but not all," Mark Prothero said of his early impressions of the case. Then, after talking with Ridgway in weekly discussions for 16 months, Prothero, too, couldn't see him as the killer. "I'm just thinking no way could this guy be responsible for killing one woman, much less 50," Prothero said.

Ridgway pleaded guilty on Nov. 5, 2003, to 48 counts of aggravated first-degree murder, accepting responsibility for the slayings of 42 women and girls on the official Green River victim list and adding six killings that police had never connected to the case. Those six included victims in 1990 and 1998, murders that happened long after many believed that the killer had died or moved away.

"I never saw that anger that was deep within him. On the surface, he maintained a normalcy, a polite demeanor that was quite the opposite of what you would expect," Prothero said. "I thought, this guy is either the world's luckiest serial killer or the world's most unlucky patronizer of prostitutes."

Indeed, Savage said Ridgway was "someone you could sit down and have a beer with in a bar and not have any clue that something's wrong with him."

Friday, Nov. 30, 2001

A year and a half before he first confessed, Ridgway was arrested and charged with four killings, based on DNA and circumstantial evidence.

Prosecutors sought the death penalty. His attorneys told Ridgway early on they would try to poke holes in the DNA evidence. As defense attorneys know, semen found in the body of a dead woman doesn't prove that person killed her. It just proves the person had sex with her. But the attorneys also told Ridgway that if one more forensic link came up that could link him to just one more Green River victim, he would be in dire straits.

Thursday, March 27, 2003

On the day King County Superior Court Judge Richard Jones set as the deadline to file any more charges against Ridgway, the defense team didn't know what would happen. Perhaps prosecutors would charge him with the remaining 45 homicides. Perhaps they wouldn't charge him with anything else. The defense attorneys based their ideas on what they knew. But none of them knew about the paint.

Prosecutors had sent hundreds of items to public and private laboratories around the country to get tests done and locate more evidence in preparation for the deadline. Because many of the remains of the Green River victims were found so long after their disappearances that only bones were left, their chances of getting much more physical evidence were slim. But they hit pay dirt with results from Microtrace, a lab in Illinois. Tests done there found tiny spheres of sprayed paint on the clothing of two young women, including Wendy Coffield, the first known victim in the Green River case. The chemical composition of the paint was identical to the highly specialized DuPont Imron paint used at the Kenworth plant where Ridgway worked.

Prosecutors charged Ridgway with three more killings, bringing the total to seven.

While defense attorney Anthony Savage still defended his client publicly, saying "What they think they can prove and what they can prove are two different things," the defense team knew their client was closer to a lethal injection. Prothero admitted the evidence was a complete surprise. It was also disturbing. Ridgway must have killed at least some of the women. "Then there was no doubt in my mind that there was not going to be an explanation that was gonna satisfy in my mind the presence of these paint spheres," he said.

What should the defense team do? "We kind of reconvened and stuck our tail between our legs and went and commiserated," Prothero said. "The strategy would be that I would begin to confront Gary about the reality of the state's evidence and the reality of our chances at trial." The team also got together to talk about "Plan B." Could they get Ridgway to talk to them about the killings? Could they persuade King County Prosecutor Norm Maleng to back down from his stance that no one deserved the death penalty more than their client? Could they save his life?

"Here's a client who said he's not guilty, and a prosecutor saying he'd never plea bargain the death penalty," Prothero said. Chances seemed slim.

Prothero started visiting Ridgway four to five times a week, in three- to four-hour sessions. At the same time, Shaw, who had been the team's connection with Ridgway's family, began talking to him about trying to get the death penalty off the table. On April 9, Ridgway agreed to think about it.

On April 10, Ridgway told his attorneys that he was responsible for several "clusters" of victims, including the first ones found at the Green River. But he "wasn't quite ready to let it all out at that point," Prothero said.

The following day, it was a resigned Ridgway who solved the 20-year mystery. He was the Green River killer. Prothero praised his client for getting the secret off his chest. "I told him it was going to help some victims' families and possibly gonna save his life." If they could plea bargain to avoid the death penalty, the odds of him living went from about 1 in 1,000 to 1 in 500. There was still a long way to go.

Monday, April 14, 2003

The defense met with Senior Deputy Prosecutor Jeff Baird, the lead prosecutor on Ridgway's case, and asked if there was room to talk. The attorneys wanted to know if the possibility existed of trading information about the murders, nearly every woman on the Green River list and some police didn't even know about, for Ridgway's life. Baird said he would get back to them.

Tuesday, April 29, 2003

The defense team met with Maleng. They didn't have much hope. In fact, they thought this was where the door to Ridgway's possible salvation would close. "He told us flat out, 'I don't do this.' " But Maleng added: "But to say no without giving it fair consideration in a case of this magnitude with this many victims and families affected, I want to talk to my top people and give it fair consideration before I make a decision." It was left unresolved. But the defense had hope. "We were thrilled on the inside, frankly," Prothero recalled. But was a deal really possible?

"We waited and we waited and we waited. Someone said it was three weeks, but to us it seemed like three years," Prothero said. "We were pretty much kept in the dark as to what their discussions were about." The defense attorneys had a feeling that the detectives in the case, and Sheriff Dave Reichert, were receptive to the idea. They wanted to end the two-decade investigation and give answers to the families of the women and girls, some of whose remains had never been found. But what would Maleng, whose statement about never bargaining with the death penalty had been broadcast at least across the state, decide?

Wednesday, June 4, 2003
The defense learned Maleng would make a deal possible. There would be serious conditions, including that Ridgway give up everything he knew and did.

Joy and relief were the feelings among the team that day. "But we weren't clinking our glasses saying the deal was done, let's go home," Prothero recalled. The attorneys went to Ridgway's cell at the King County Jail and told him the news. "As with other aspects of this case, my emotional reaction to what was going on was probably more than Gary's," Prothero said. "I think Gary's emotional range is blunted. He was relieved and pleased, but it wasn't like he was overjoyed and jumping up and down with happiness." In fact, the most demanding part lay ahead of him — recounting the crimes.

Friday, June 13, 2003
Ridgway signed the paperwork for the plea agreement. He was then moved away from the jail, to a secret, secure location, the Green River Task Force headquarters at Boeing Field. There the detectives, Reichert and various experts could talk with him at length on a daily basis. He was questioned extensively. The days lasted "10, 12, 14 hours" in one estimation. There were interviews and evaluations by a forensic psychologist who specializes in serial, sexual murders. The FBI sent in an expert for six hours of interviews, and Reichert talked with Ridgway one-on-one for 16 hours.

There were excursions to victim dump sites identified by the killer. He didn't know their names or remember many faces. But he knew critical details, mostly precisely where he left his victims' bodies. "It's bizarre," Prothero said. "There's no other way to explain it. It's just strange and sick and twisted."

Ridgway went to the sites with police and his attorneys. At some places they found nothing. But over the next five months, the remains of four victims were located. They were the first remains found in the case in more than a decade.

Saturday, June 14, 2003, to Tuesday, Nov. 4, 2003

Ridgway discussed much with police and others throughout this period, including why he temporarily stopped killing and why he killed in the first place. For years, Ridgway felt he might never be caught, but police came too close in 1987. That's when they did an intensive search of his home and took hair and saliva samples from him. That may have saved lives.

He married his third wife, Judith, the following year. The marriage may have contributed to his slowing or stopping his murderous spree. "He loved Judith very much," Prothero said. "It kind of took him away and gave him pleasure and took his mind off of the darker things that gave him pleasure. It enabled him to slow down and stop to have this other life that was fulfilling to him." There was also Peaches the poodle. The couple took Peaches and other dogs they owned throughout their marriage on long walks and Ridgway told police that cut into his time to cruise and/or kill.

Even so, Ridgway admitted he "fell off the wagon and killed" in 1990 and 1998, and police surveillance showed that he continued to patrol for prostitutes until he was arrested in November 2001. The double life he led during those years may have compounded the problem of recounting the killings, but not everyone involved in those interviews believe the lapses in his memory are legitimate.

"He told lies and lived lies just as a matter of course, so even the things that he's digging out, it's difficult to know if that's something he conjured up and stuck in there as part of his ongoing existence," Prothero said. "What I believe is that his brain has been badly miswired."

But Prothero said the most compelling answers are yet to come.

"Why did this happen? What went wrong in his life that maybe we can learn and be more aware of the warning signs? I think we've only scratched the surface with Gary as to his childhood." Prothero added that without the death of Ridgway's mother, Mary, on Aug. 15, 2001, Ridgway might never have confessed. "Just the impression I get from him, he would've rather died than have his mother know that he was the killer."

Part II: Verification

Every murder that Ridgway confessed to had to be verified.

The simplest cases were those in which bodies had been recovered and identified. Since there was no physical evidence linking Ridgway to most of the murders, that usually meant Ridgway had to produce information that only the killer could know. This process was crucial, given that misattributing a murder to Ridgway would mean the real killer would never be caught.

Cases with unidentified bodies were more difficult, since police themselves had little information to go on. But the most difficult were cases in which no body was recovered. In order for there to be a crime, there has to be a victim, and in many cases, Ridgway could offer only random details. He had killed so many women over so many years that it was hard to keep them straight. Nearly all the victims — more than 60 by his estimation — were anonymous to him. He didn't know their names, and he rarely remembered a face. Sometimes he recalled a pattern of clothing or a piece of jewelry. He often mixed up dates, sometimes placing his crimes years before or after they occurred. The one thing he tended to remember is where he dumped a victim.

By housing Ridgway at the Task Force headquarters at Boeing Field in south Seattle, investigators were closer to investigation sites and better able to come and go without being noticed.

Ridgway spent five months at that location, a nondescript 10- by 12-square-foot room in an office building, furnished with a mattress and box spring. Strips of black electrical tape covered the power outlets. The walls were painted mostly an office beige. The blue-gray carpet was the same his captors walked on just a few feet away. A motion sensor was aware of Ridgway's every move, and he was under 24-hour video monitoring. To bathe, he used a "camping shower" filled with hot water. He was escorted to the bathroom. The door to the room was removed, replaced by a table where Ridgway would sit and watch the mostly vacant area immediately in front of his room. He would share greetings with detectives. He was never allowed to wander unescorted through the Green River Task Force's headquarters.

Detective Jon Mattsen talked about the process leading up to off-site visits. Detectives would interview Ridgway two at a time, on topics developed in advance. The interviews took place in a long rectangular room, watched over by at least one member of Ridgway's defense team. Ridgway sat in a hard plastic chair at a round table, facing a wall where the detectives' PowerPoint presentations were displayed. Detectives had a system of punishments and rewards — including a special one, a takeout salmon dinner. Next door was the detectives' command center of sorts, where they would gather to feed questions via an intranet connection to those who were interviewing Ridgway at the table.

Many of the rumors that were reported in the press during this time were false. Ridgway wasn't living in a three-room apartment, and he had not gone to Western State Hospital for a mental evaluation. There had been an evaluation, but it had been done right there, at the Task Force headquarters. In October, when stormwater flooded the headquarters and threatened to damage evidence, Ridgway was moved to another secure location that authorities kept secret.

During his five months at the Task Force headquarters, detectives escorted Ridgway to dump sites on 24 occasions and scoured 51 sites, including the ravine on busy Kent-Des Moines Road where the remains of an unidentified victim were found. Never once did they catch the media's attention while Ridgway was with them. Ridgway also was taken to Lake Fenwick on Kent's West Hill in August, where detectives cleared about five acres. According to Task Force spokeswoman Kathleen Larson, Ridgway was adamant "he put somebody there." Nothing was found.

When Ridgway was transported to investigation sites, it was often in the company of the man who pursued him starting as a young detective in 1982, King County Sheriff Dave Reichert. Reichert said it was an "eerie feeling" to have Ridgway at his side at locations where victims were dumped. It also took a strong stomach. Ridgway enjoyed returning to his "clusters" of bodies, and the detectives were helping him indulge his fantasy.

"That was hard for us," Reichert said after a press conference the day after Ridgway's guilty plea. Sometimes, to get needed information, Reichert said, a detective has "to be the best friend to a person you absolutely despise." At one site, as Reichert watched,

Ridgway stopped precisely where 16-year-old Mary West's remains had been found 18 years earlier. "It sent chills up my spine," Reichert said.

Part III: Preparation

Prosecutors knew their decision to bargain away the death penalty would be controversial. Before the plea bargain became public, Maleng and Reichert laid the groundwork for explaining the context and thinking behind the deal and, with the participation of Judge Jones, scripted the day in court.

To show unity, Maleng and Reichert planned a joint press conference that would take place immediately after the court hearing. They also wrote a joint statement, to be released as soon as details of the deal became public. After recounting the investigation, the statement addressed the death-penalty decision head-on:

"The decision to set aside the death penalty in return for full disclosure and investigative assistance presented a collision of important principles. On one hand was the longstanding policy in the prosecuting attorney's office that the death penalty was not a plea-bargaining tool. What the agreement in this case offered, however, was another bedrock principle of justice: the opportunity to know the truth. It offered victimized families the answers to haunting questions, and could close a chapter in our country's history that cried out for closure."

Everything was now in place for the day in court.

Elaine Thompson
Gary Ridgway hears charges, flanked by defense attorneys Mark Prothero, left, and Anthony Savage.

Guilty
Chapter 21
Part I: The Hearing

NOV. 5, 2003.

Many of the relatives of Green River victims had been waiting for this day for more than 20 years. So had investigators, prosecutors, media, court officials and the entire community. The largest courtroom in Seattle's King County Courthouse had been wired for live television and most of the seats were reserved for the families of victims. Judge Richard Jones presided. Every detail of the day was scripted, from the moment the building opened at 6 a.m. through to the final press conference.

Over the previous three days, Sheriff Dave Reichert, victim advocate Mary Kirchner and sometimes Prosecutor Norm Maleng met with every family of Green River victims and presumed victims. It was here, in these private meetings, that they were allowed to cry, rage, ask questions and get answers. Many expressed their appreciation for being contacted personally. There were more than 50 such meetings. The families were briefed on legal proceedings and logistics and issued Sheriff's Office business cards. The cards identified them as family members and gave them access to a private room on the eighth floor, and from there to the ninth floor courtroom where the hearing would begin at 9 a.m.

Family members began arriving shortly after the courthouse opened and passed through the first level of security. Some talked quietly with reporters. Others went directly to the family-only room on the eighth floor, complete with refreshments and closed-circuit television. From the eighth floor, they were given the choice of being escorted up a back staircase or going through the hallway, where they would have a chance to talk with the press. Some braved the TV and still cameras and reporters crowded outside the courtroom. Reichert swept through the same way, barely noticed by the cameras.

By 8 a.m., many family members had already taken their seats. Word had leaked to the press that Gary Ridgway would plead guilty to killing 48 women and girls, but he had yet to do so in open court. Family members — parents, husbands, sisters, brothers, children — wanted to be able to see and hear when he finally said the word, as he did, 48 times. "Guilty."

The audience was seated when Ridgway walked in, wearing a bulletproof vest beneath bright-red prison coveralls. He was surrounded by guards and two of his attorneys, Savage and Prothero. Judge Jones kept a tight rein on the demeanor of everyone in his court. There were no taunts, no gasps. There was such a tone of dignity and solemnity that Maleng later compared the proceedings to a memorial service. Tears flowed when the names of Ridgway's victims were read. Some left the courtroom, overcome by the grief — and some by anger. For many it was the first time to see the killer in person.

Reporters were also warned about appropriate behavior and were given 48-page information packets that included general policies, a case summary, rules for cameras, orders on media coverage, the original charges against Ridgway and a biography on Jones. Reporters were warned that if the judge or deputies even saw a telephone or pager, even if it was turned off, it would be taken away until the hearing was over.

Senior Deputy Prosecutor Jeff Baird opened the questioning of Ridgway, summarizing the case and mentioning the names of the women, the dates they disappeared or were likely killed, and where their bodies were dumped. That lasted 37 minutes.

Then it was time for Ridgway to rise and face Judge Jones, who asked Ridgway how he pleaded to each murder. Ridgway began in a strong voice, his face impassive. At Count 17 — the murder of Constance Naon — his voice lost some of its strength. He blinked rapidly. Two counts later, he swiped his nose and sniffed audibly. Ridgway seemed to recover, but at Count 31 — Debbie Abernathy — Prothero leaned forward: "Are you OK?" Ridgway nodded. By Count 46, the murder of Mary E. West, Ridgway appeared near tears. Then it was over. He sat down and looked straight ahead. He was back in control. In just 8$_{1/2}$ minutes, Ridgway had pleaded guilty to 48 counts of aggravated murder.

Forty-four families now know who killed their daughters. But four families weren't there. They remain unknown, just like the remains of four of Ridgway's victims, identified in court as Jane Doe B-10, Jane Doe B-16, Jane Doe B-17 and Jane Doe B-20. Also in attendance were family members related to victims previously attributed to the Green River killer but not included in the plea bargain: Amina Agisheff, Kase Lee, Rebecca Marrero, Tammie Liles, Keli McGinness and Patricia Osborn.

About an hour and 40 minutes after it began, the hearing ended with Jones making several announcements about upcoming press conferences. First to leave was Ridgway and his defense team. He was escorted out a side door by a phalanx of police officers. He walked by Reichert. Their eyes didn't meet.

Patrick Hagerty

Sarah Christensen holds up a childhood photo of herself and her mother, Carol Ann Christensen, before Carol became a victim of the Green River Killer in 1983. Sarah was 5 years old when her mother disappeared.

Gary Ridgway: The Green River Killer 157

Matt Brashears

Patrick Hagerty

Kathy Mills speaks with reporters after Ridgway pleaded guilty to the murder of her daughter, Opal Mills.

Opal Mills

Shirley Sherrill

Rosemary Fries, middle, reacts as Marilyn Molina, right, speaks about her sister, Marie Malvar. Marie and Fries' daughter, Shirley Sherrill, were both killed by Ridgway.

David Nelson

Patricia Barczak is comforted by an unidentified friend after confirming that her daughter, also named Patricia Barczak, was killed by Ridgway.

Patricia Barczak

158   Gary Ridgway: The Green River Killer

Patrick Hagerty

The portrait of Debra Estes, 15 years old when she was slain by Ridgway, rests in a seat by her mother, Carol Estes, and sister, Virginia Graham, during a press conference of family members of Green River killer victims.

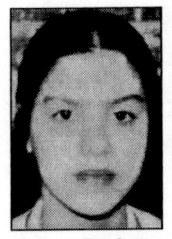

Perfecto Marrero is the brother of Becky Marrero, above, whose body has never been found. Gary Ridgway did not confess to her murder, but is considered a prime suspect.

Gary Kissel

Part II: Remembering the Victims

When court proceedings ended, the families of victims came forward to tell their stories, speaking both for themselves and for those silenced by death.

They miss their daughters' laughter, their dimples. They miss the chances they never had to make their mom proud with good grades and new jobs. They miss the chances they didn't get to share the delights of becoming a mother or an aunt. They miss their best friends. They miss their mothers.

The families expressed many kinds of loss after the Green River killer was convicted. Parents, children, sisters and brothers, aunts and uncles gathered at a local city hall to share their family memories and talk about Gary Leon Ridgway, the man who changed their lives forever.

"I am in complete agreement with the prosecuting attorney's office where the plea is concerned. Frankly, I think death is too good for Gary Ridgway ... I'd like to think his life in prison will be a living hell," said Mertie Winston, mother of Tracy Winston, who was 19 when Ridgway killed her and dumped her near the Green River in Kent in 1983. Winston pointed out the painfully short distance between her family and Ridgway's carnage. Tracy's remains were found in Cottonwood Park, not far from the Winston family home. And several other victims were found in a park where Tracy and her brothers played baseball when they were kids. Mertie Winston and her husband used to work in the building now used as the headquarters for the Green River Task Force.

Tracy, in fact, knew Ridgway before he picked her up in September 1983, her mother said, which most certainly made her more vulnerable to him because of Tracy's trusting, loyal personality. "I miss the fact that I never got to know her as an adult," Winston said. "I resent Ridgway for taking that away from me. But I don't hate him. If I hate him, then he takes a part of me that I don't want to give up ... he won't get another ounce of feeling from me."

Sarah Christensen lives her life with another kind of loss. Sarah was 5 when her mother, Carol Christensen, was killed at the age of 21. "For me, this is a different experience. ... It was hard because I grew up without my mom." Sarah's mental pictures of picking cherries and making daisy chains in the back yard with her mom are as vivid to her as if they'd shared that time together yesterday. So is the memory of showing up at her mother's house for a weekend visit to find her not at home. And clear is the memory of her grandfather telling Sarah that her mother wasn't coming back. Christensen, now an orthodontist's assistant, honors her mother's memory by trying to be the best person she can be. "I think she'd be really proud of me."

Carol Estes and Virginia Graham, mother and sister to Green River murder victim Debra Estes, held a color drawing of her as they talked about their beloved Debra, killed at the age of 15. Three years older than her sister, Graham remembers sticking up for her sister in every situation when they were teenagers. "If somebody ever hurt her, I was always the first one there," Graham said. "Except for this time."

Graham was 18 when Debra walked out the door at 3 p.m. on Sept. 20, 1982, heading for Pacific Highway South. Debra was found six years later by construction workers at two apartment buildings at South 348th Street and First Avenue South in Federal Way. "I am an only child at this point, and I miss my sister a lot." Since her sister's disappearance, Graham said, she's been stunned at the implication that Green River victims were partly at fault in their own murders because many of them were prostitutes.

Others echoed her feelings. "These were young women who were deserving of our society's help, not criticisms," said Mertie Winston. Some of the women had their difficulties, "but they did not deserve to die." Deanna Fries said her sister, Shirley Sherrill, was human "regardless of what she did for a living."

Tim Meehan's family lost two people the day Ridgway killed Mary Meehan, 18, who was more than seven months pregnant. He is sympathetic and realistic about the victims and the situations that put them in the path of a man preying on prostitutes.

The victims often shielded their families from the details of their lives, knowing the worries and trouble they would cause, and many of them died without ever resolving strained family relationships. The mother of Patricia Barczak was fortunate in that respect. Patricia, who had lived and worked in Bellevue, was 19 when she vanished near the airport in October 1986. But shortly before she disappeared, a poignant moment passed between mother and daughter, who share the name Patricia. "She said 'Mom, I'm sorry for all the trouble I've caused. And I want you to know I love you.' "

Patricia's skull was found in 1993 by a survey crew working along Highway 18 in Auburn.

For many of the victims' family members, watching Ridgway plead guilty to the murders of 48 women was more than they could bear. The emotions of their loss resurfaced, as fresh and raw as they were the day their sisters, mothers and daughters disappeared, the day they got the phone call identifying their remains. Family members choked up as they spoke or let the tears roll as they listened to the familiar stories of those sitting next to them. For them, this was a day to release emotions that had built up over 20 years. Others, by some power, were composed as they described their greatest loss, their worst nightmare.

Helen Dexter talked about Constance Naon, her only daughter out of seven children, who disappeared in June 1983. "It devastated my boys. And I love my boys, but I really miss my girl." For years after the disappearance of "Connie," Dexter found herself buying gifts for a girl, only to pack them away once she got home. There is a special relationship between a mother and daughter, Dexter said, and Ridgway denied her that relationship with Connie — Connie the beautiful young woman who wanted to be a model, the woman whose children Dexter never got to hold. To honor her daughter, and to make sure she's remembered for more than being a Green River murder victim, Dexter has set up a scholarship fund at Holy Names Academy in Seattle.

Shirley Sherrill's family was happy to have Ridgway caught and in prison, but angry that the murderer seemed to show no remorse in court. The week of Ridgway's guilty pleadings brought some firsts for the family, including their first interview about Shirley and the first time they became aware that her remains were found in two places — off Auburn-Black Diamond Road and in Tigard, Ore.

Sarah Christensen said she supports the decision to let Ridgway spend life in prison, even though her mother was one of the first four victims he was charged with killing, and Sarah had nothing to gain by Ridgway's deal. But she knows she wouldn't want to be one of the families left unable to recover their loved one's remains and excluded from Ridgway's conviction. Christensen said she wants Ridgway to suffer not physically, but emotionally. She wants him to wake up every day missing the people he loves and to know there's never going to be a day when he can again have a normal family life. "I want him to know what it feels like to have family taken away from him," Christensen said.

Jose Malvar, brother of Marie Malvar, said the 1983 disappearance of his sister broke his family apart and wrecked his parents' marriage. There is no closure after what they have been through, and he's not happy with the agreement that is allowing Ridgway to avoid the death penalty, although his sister's remains were found as a result of the plea. That didn't matter, Jose Malvar said. The family always knew Marie was a victim of the Green River killer. Jose Malvar said his only solace is the hope that Ridgway will be placed in the general population in prison, where prisoners might take matters into their own hands.

Marie Malvar and her sister Marilyn were best friends when they were growing up. When Marie was 18 and Marilyn just a year younger, the two were living together in an apartment. They were supposed to go out together one night in April, but Marilyn wasn't feeling well. With their plans canceled, Marie said she was going out just for a minute. She said she'd come right back, but she never did. Marilyn, now Marilyn Molina, moved to California shortly after her sister's disappearance. She rarely returns to Washington because the sights of the places she knew with her sister by her side are too painful, even 20 years later. Molina doesn't believe in the death penalty, but "I truly believe he will pay for what he's done."

Others spoke of closure or the lack of it. Joan Mackie, whose daughter Cindy Anne Smith, 17, was last seen hitchhiking on Pacific Highway South, said there is no justice in the decision to let Ridgway live when so many women died by his hands, and there is no peace. "There will be no closure until my daughter and I see him dead."

Sandra Gabbert, 17, disappeared April 17, 1983, the same day as Kimi-Kai Pitsor, 16. There's a connection there, said Gabbert's mother, Nancy Gabbert. She's not sure what the significance of the timing is, but she knows she'll never find out if their killer is put to death. She said it's a waste of young lives to throw away the knowledge Ridgway has in him. He is, in effect, a resource of information about what makes a serial killer.

"Fifty-four years ago, Gary Ridgway was a darling, adorable, lovable little baby. He's not some monster that dropped down on us from another planet," she said. Whatever happened to make him want to kill dozens of women happened in our society. How did it happen? "There's a lot we need to learn — an awful lot — and we're not going to learn it by killing Gary Ridgway."

For some, there are no answers.

Ridgway's conviction did nothing to resolve the anguish of the Marrero family. For mother Rebecca, daughter Mary and son Perfecto, there were no answers about their beloved Becky, who disappeared in December 1982.

"We hoped we would hear something about Becky today, but they didn't even say her name," Perfecto Marrero said. "To wait all these years, it's frustrating. We wonder where our sister is. Is she alive? Is she dead?"

The Marreros are one of seven families of presumed victims of the Green River killer who were not included in Ridgway's plea bargain. Of the seven, one set of remains has never been identified. Another, Amina Agisheff, may have been one of Ridgway's first victims. She disappeared July 7, 1982, but Ridgway cannot say for sure whether he killed her, and police lack the evidence to press the point. The story of Tammie Liles is similar. She was last seen June 9, 1983, in downtown Seattle, and her remains were found two years later in Tualatin, Ore., south of Portland, with no physical evidence linking her to Ridgway. The families of Agisheff and Liles were left out of whatever solace the other victims' families may have received from Ridgway's convictions, but at least they have a grave to visit.

Becky Marrero is one of four presumed victims of the Green River killer whose remains have never been found. The others are Kase Lee, Keli McGinness and Patricia Osborn, who have all now been missing for more than 20 years.

In his confessions, Ridgway said he believes he did kill Lee, McGinness and Osborn, but his claim has not been corroborated. He was uncertain about Marrero. In Lee's case, police are unable to search where Ridgway said he left her body because of development in the area.

In an interview before Ridgway's conviction, Mary Marrero expressed the particular grief of those families. Mary and Becky were very close, and Mary says she has thought about her sister every day of those 20 years. "It never leaves your mind," she said. Mary knows that Becky must be dead, but she can't help looking into the faces of strangers and wondering, "Is that my sister? Is that her?" She misses the older sister who gave her a cross tattoo on the back of her right hand, matching the cross Mary tattooed on Becky's left and symbolizing their inseparability. She misses Becky's sunny, generous disposition. "She had the best personality, the best sense of humor, and she was very bright. She had the kindest heart and would go out of her way to help anybody rather than help herself." She remembers how much Becky loved spending time with her daughter, now 24, and going to area beaches with her sister and friends.

In 1982, Mary was 15 and pregnant. It was a low point in her life, and she wanted to turn things around. She left home for California, intending to start life anew with the baby she was carrying. Then Becky disappeared and Mary came home. "Nobody knew nothing. She just disappeared. ... Mom had a nervous breakdown after that."

Mary understands. In addition to losing Becky, she now shares with her mother the terrible bond of losing a child. Her second daughter, 17-year-old Josie Peterson, was murdered on March 9, 2001. Also killed were Josie's boyfriend, Taelor Marks, also 17, and Marks' grandparents, Dick and Jane Larson. The four were shot, stabbed and/or bludgeoned to death in the Larsons' home in Des Moines, south of Seattle. The man charged with the killings — Leemah Carneh, 20, of Pierce County — has not yet gone to trial, and no firm date has been set.

"Sometimes, you think, 'Why me? Why do I have to go through it?'" Like her mother, Mary has become emotionally fragile. "I don't think there's enough counseling to get over this. You just don't overcome it. ... I stay home all the time, because I am so insecure of the world."

Mary has seen the photos of victims many times, and sat in court with row after row of their loved ones. She thinks about all of them and the hundreds more they represent. "There are whole generations that will never be the same," she said. "Think of all the moms, the dads, the sisters, the brothers, the cousins, the relatives all messed up because of him. There's people who went off the deep end over this. Some of them may have even killed themselves, we don't know."

Then she thinks about what she still has. "I look at the children I have left. I look at my niece, and that's what gives me strength to live. I want them to have a better life than me."

Elaine Thompson
In court, on the day he was
convicted of 48 murders.

The Mind of a Killer
Chapter 22

IF GARY RIDGWAY HAD BEEN WEARING a suit and tie the day he pleaded guilty, you would have been hard-pressed to pick out the serial killer among the row of attorneys.

Looking into his eyes would have yielded nothing. No hint of any inner torment, no sign of rage, no mark of evil — nothing to distinguish him from anyone else. Call it a poker face. Looking at this 54-year-old man, or even talking with him, gives no clue of what he called his career, the strangulation of young women and girls.

If you asked Gary Ridgway why he killed more than 60 women over a 20- to 30-year period, he would tell you many things.

He told investigators people would write books about him and that he wanted to portray himself in the best possible light. He told them he had not planned to kill any of his victims, that he killed in a rage when his "dates" with prostitutes went wrong.

He said his anger came from a variety of sources: work (where women manipulated others to get the easier jobs); his purchase of a home (all the light bulbs were removed before he moved in); late payments by his tenants; his divorces; poor sleep; failure to stick up for himself; child support payments.

He said that killing released the pressure of these and other problems.

"Eventually, he acknowledged that many of these claims were false," prosecutors wrote, "and he admitted that once he managed to get a woman to his house, he killed her, regardless of how she acted or how he felt."

That he changed his stories and seemed uncertain about the truth isn't unusual for serial killers. Some confess to killings they didn't commit and some keep slayings to themselves.

"Ridgway greatly minimized his behavior and acknowledged that he was a pathological liar. In candid moments, Ridgway acknowledged that it was difficult for him to be truthful, after being so successfully deceptive about the killings for decades," prosecutors wrote in court documents that summarized his crimes.

Prosecutors found Ridgway's memory problems "highly selective." Although he said he couldn't remember names or faces, he knew details of where he left bodies and could provide amazingly accurate accounts of every vehicle he ever owned, his residences and his work history, including which shifts he had worked over the years. "In particular, Ridgway demonstrated an extraordinary memory for those things which meant something to him — particularly, his possessions and how much he paid for them."

Defense attorney Mark Prothero, who has spent more time with Ridgway than anyone else connected to the case, said deception had become part of his client's nature. "He lived this kind of duality most of his adult life. He told lies and lived lies just as a matter of course."

Robert Keppel, who assisted in the Green River investigation, is one of the nation's foremost experts on serial murders. He has interviewed serial killers, studied them, hunted them and consulted with police on their cases. Because serial killers haven't been studied in a clinical setting, he also knows that there are many things we don't know about them.

Keppel has a doctorate in philosophy and teaches classes on serial murder, criminal investigation and techniques in crime scene investigation at Sam Houston State University in Texas. He worked for the King County Police Department, now known as the King County

Sheriff's Office, from January 1971 to March 1982, spending his last eight years as a homicide detective.

From January 1983 to 1998, Keppel worked as chief consultant to the department on the Green River killings while he was chief criminal investigator for the Washington State Attorney General's Office. He and then-King County Detective Dave Reichert interviewed serial killer Ted Bundy, who had grown up in Tacoma, earned a psychology degree from the University of Washington and started his string of killings in the Seattle area.

"He's not telling all," Keppel said when asked about Ridgway. "Now I'm not going to call him a liar, but what I think we have going here is a full-blown psychopathic killer, a real lust killer."

Such lust killers, Keppel said, have a "lack of affect." He described it as "a deadpan look, deadpan enunciation, deadpan sentence structure, no emotion, no remorse, no empathy in the interview situation, everything seems as though it's been dehumanized."

He saw that in Bundy, who confessed to killing 30 women, but was convicted only of three and was executed in Florida in 1989. He saw it in John Gacy, executed in 1994 for killing 33 men and boys and hiding them in the crawl space under his home in Chicago in the early 1970s. He saw it in Jack Spillman, an East Wenatchee, Wash., laborer who raped, murdered and mutilated three females, including a 9-year-old girl. Spillman is serving life without the possibility of parole in a Washington prison.

"These are people who are loaded with an absolute lack of affect in everything they do," Keppel said. "They can't tolerate intimacy or socialize in any way other than their predatory nature."

Serial killers, he added, "have this chameleon capability where they can change their whole approach, their appearances, depending on their advantages to avoid being the prey, if you will, and have success as the predator."

Keppel speculates that Ridgway might have been telling detectives just what he knew they wanted to hear. Or he might have told them things he knew would keep them satisfied, so he could keep many more details to himself.

He had done it before. Detectives contacted Ridgway several times during their investigation — nearly a dozen times — and he passed a polygraph test in 1984. They even followed him on Pacific Highway South in the mid-1980s while he cruised for prostitutes, but the surveillance netted nothing.

"He adopted the same unremarkable, non-threatening affect he used to lull his victims into complacency to avoid bringing himself to the attention of law enforcement," prosecutors wrote in their summary. "When interviewed by the Task Force, his apparent forthrightness and willingness to cooperate was disarming. Ridgway would admit everything he believed the Task Force already knew about him, and just a little bit more."

When questioned, he admitted to police that he dated prostitutes, saying he was addicted to them like an alcoholic is to drink. The police would go away satisfied that he was an ordinary john.

In 1984, when he passed the polygraph test that temporarily cleared him as a suspect in the slayings, he had already killed dozens of women and young girls. "By agreeing to be interviewed without an attorney, and to take a polygraph examination, Ridgway avoided suspicion all the more," prosecutors noted.

In fact, Ridgway likely used this same disarming technique on his victims as well. "He knew car date prostitutes like the back of his hand. Killers like him have a survivability. They can say or do something to make these people feel slightly satisfied," Keppel explained.

At this point, Ridgway may not even know the truth himself, Keppel said.

"If you look at the prosecution documents, the detectives had one hell of a time trying to interview him. Not that he's intentionally lying. But let's face it, these people are such good liars, they don't even know themselves when they're lying."

Ridgway did tell the truth about some things. Police verified that.

"As part of the process of testing his claim to be the Green River killer, Ridgway led the police to the places he left bodies and described what he did there. His memory for these locations surpassed all the information provided to his attorneys and the knowledge of detectives who had worked on the case. In addition, he identified several dump sites on cases that were never considered Green River cases; information about these cases had not been provided to the defense," prosecutors wrote.

Four sets of human remains were found at those sites. Three of them have been identified as Green River victims who had been missing since the 1980s.

As some serial killers do, Ridgway talked of an abnormal relationship with his mother, Mary. He told detectives that he was sexually attracted to her and that his feelings for her were a mixture of lust and admiration. He had vivid memories of his mother washing his genitals, something she did into his teens, he said.

But no one has verified those stories. His mother died in August 2001, just three months before he was arrested and charged with four killings. His father, Thomas Ridgway, died in January 1998.

Keppel said taking Ridgway's claims at face value doesn't help anyone. "He can say anything he wants. You have no way to corroborate any of this stuff."

Ridgway could be playing psychiatric and psychological games for the detectives. "He knows it turns the lights on in some people. People will say, 'Aha, his mother was terrible to him.' But he may be saying it just to be saying it."

In other words, it could all be lies.

"He's changing his stories. He's not telling the whole truth all the way through. It's not something he can come up with in a clear and concise manner," Keppel said. "So it's hard for the detectives to handle this guy, because he handles everything. He's got such experience from 20 years or more of killing and deceiving about killing."

It may be we'll never know how much of what Ridgway told detectives is true.

• • •

Why?

That's what people want to know when someone is murdered. And that's what people want to know about Ridgway now.

Why did he choose the victims he did? What was he thinking when he killed? Why did he kill over and over again?

What turned Ridgway from a gap-toothed child into a cold-blooded killer who had sex with victims after he killed them?

For some people, answers to such questions provide comfort. For those who study killers, the answers can shed light on warning signs for future cases. But Keppel said those answers may never come. "The only thing you can say about him is that he liked to kill."

Researchers want answers that fit all serial killers. All-purpose answers, if you will. But does anyone really have those answers?

Keppel says no.

"Some of them are so involved with fantasy life there's not any sense in going to talk to them," he said of serial killers in general. "They haven't been studied anywhere in a group situation, nothing like, 'Here's a block of 30 serial killers. Here's their brain scans, their biological problems.' We just don't know that stuff about any of them.

"I know that Bundy didn't know why he killed. At least he said he didn't."

Ridgway did tell investigators that he hated women, hated prostitutes. Was he being truthful, or was he saying that because it's one of the things people easily believe about serial killers? He said he "never gave a thought to how the victims felt while he was killing them." Asked by a forensic psychologist if he thought there was something missing in him that was present in other people, Ridgway replied: 'Caring.'

"It's, I didn't, the women's faces don't, don't mean anything to me. There were, the bodies, if they had a, had a pussy, I would screw and that was it."

But he did care about where he put his victims, and about losing them to the detectives and others who found their remains. He told police in his confessions that when "his" bodies were found, he felt like someone was taking something away from him.

Prothero said he doesn't think his client knows why he killed: "There is no pat answer to the 'why' question. It's down in some deep and twisted recesses of his mind. Why on Earth does someone like to kill? That's the deeper question, and I think the answer lies deep within Gary's brain and others like him.

"He doesn't know why he wanted to kill prostitutes," Prothero said. "I don't think he's intentionally withholding an answer to the why questions. I think he wonders like everyone else."

•••

Gary Ridgway didn't know Ted Bundy, but it seems Bundy sure knew Ridgway. Keppel wrote a book about the two men: "The Riverman — Ted Bundy and I Hunt for the Green River Killer."

Keppel now says: "If you went to 'The Riverman' and pulled out every thing Bundy said about the Riverman, it was 100 percent true, with one exception. He thought he lived in Pierce County. He lived in

South King County. That's the only thing he missed."

In 1974, when the killings began in Washington state that were later linked to Bundy, Ridgway was a 25-year-old newlywed living near the Sea-Tac Strip. That they came from the same area, were about the same age, and killed a decade apart, is something people love to talk about, but they didn't know one another.

But even without knowing Ridgway, Bundy came to know *about* him. He wrote the Task Force from his Florida prison cell on death row and offered to help catch the killer. Bundy said he would only talk with Keppel, who had helped track his own killing spree.

"Bundy had a deeper understanding of serial killers than most people do," Keppel said. "He had studied all the studies, read all the books, committed the murders himself, talked with other killers on death row in Florida. He probably had a knowledge base far greater than ours."

Bundy said the Green River killer "is fairly well composed and, generally speaking, a normal guy."

Ridgway seemed proud of appearing normal. The women and girls he picked up saw a father, with toys on the dash of his truck. They saw a slightly built, even thin, guy. Women asked him if he was the killer and he would ask in return:

"Uh, do I look like the Green River killer?"

Ridgway "cultivated the innocuous aspects of his personality — his nonthreatening, unimpressive appearance, meek demeanor, and small stature," prosecutors wrote. "In this way he conned scores of victims who had survived years using street smarts."

Ridgway was also cool under pressure. An expert tracker who analyzed the area where one victim was found said the body had been concealed "by one man, who made repeated, calm, and organized trips from the body to a brush pile and back, made no wasted movements, and showed no signs of panic."

Bundy said people had seen the killer, possibly even as he picked up his victims, but no one thought anything of it.

"There's no question in my mind that you have eyewitnesses all over, people who saw this guy and just don't know what they've seen," he told Keppel and Reichert during their visit to Florida. "He is well composed, and he knows how to approach those people. He knows how to limit the risks, but there's not a way to *eliminate* the risks. And, he's able to do it. The main reason he's been so successful, apart from his own canniness and wariness, is the fact of the kind of victims he's dealing with."

The reason police didn't have "anything really reliable is, because any time you have a space of days or weeks before the victim is reported missing and no publicity about the disappearance, there ain't nobody coming forward," Bundy said.

All true.

Ridgway told police in his confessions that he picked prostitutes and runaways because he knew no one would miss them quickly, if at all. His assessment was correct, prosecutors wrote in their summary.

"Police were often delayed in their investigation because no missing person report was filed, and, even when a disappearance was reported, it was difficult for investigators to pin down where the victim had last been seen. Complicating matters were numerous alleged sightings of the 'missing' victims long after they had been killed."

People did see Ridgway with women who later turned up missing. He told a psychologist during his confession that those were mistakes he made. But at the time he was able to explain it away. And people also saw him with women who didn't disappear. He would go on some dates and return the women unharmed. This built trust; some of those women vouched for him when talking with other prostitutes.

In fact, Ridgway told police he believed people at a 7-Eleven on the Strip knew him as "a steady customer" of prostitutes. He would meet women in the parking lot there and make arrangements to meet them elsewhere so he could pick them up without others noticing.

Bundy said the killer was likely choosing his victims with care.

"I have to say this guy is in and out and closely observing his victims, if not all the time in the area, at least a particular victim for some period of time. He's going to a great deal of trouble to check out the area, and everything that goes on in that area," Bundy told Keppel and Reichert.

"He's very conscious of the police. I bet you he can feel them, undercover or whatever, because he's very conscious of not wanting to have anybody observe him approach one of those girls, but also because, you know, he's lived in that scene long enough; he knows what they look like."

Ridgway told investigators he spent hours "patrolling," his term for looking for victims. In fact, he sometimes slept just a few hours per night so that he could spend more time watching and waiting, killing victims and disposing of their bodies.

Bundy said he didn't think the Riverman killed victim Amina Agisheff. She was older than other victims at the time, and she didn't have any known links to prostitution. She was a 35-year-old mother of three who was returning home to her kids when she disappeared. Ridgway told police that he didn't kill Agisheff. Her slaying remains unsolved, and she remains on the Task Force's Green River victims' list.

Ridgway told police he preyed on younger women because they were relatively innocent and less likely to con him than women in their twenties. He also said younger women talked more when they were dying, pleading earnestly for their lives.

Bundy said the killer had ways to get the women to trust him. In fact, ruses had worked well for Bundy himself, who once put one arm in a sling to get women to feel sorry enough to help him. Ridgway told prostitutes he'd become a regular customer, lend them his vehicles, get them jobs, feed them. He'd tell them about his son — surely this doting father wasn't the Green River killer.

Bundy also said one thing the killer had going for him was that he didn't talk to anyone about the murders. He didn't need to. Prosecutors acknowledged that Ridgway had "a remarkable ability to remain silent" and that helped him elude police all those years.

Until learning of the evidence behind his 2001 arrest, his family knew nothing of the killings, other than that he had been a suspect years before. His wife, Judith, said their relationship was excellent. Even after Ridgway confessed, one of his brothers said Ridgway had never shown any abnormal behavior.

In their discussions in the 1980s, Reichert asked Bundy if he thought it was possible for the Green River killer to stop.

"No! Not unless he was born again and got filled with the Holy Spirit in a very real way. He's either moved, he's dead, or he's doing something very different," Bundy said.

Ridgway hadn't stopped. But he did slow down after a frenzied killing spree in the early 1980s. Keppel said he believed that the 1987 search of Ridgway's home put a scare into him and convinced him to stop killing for a time.

Bundy thought the killer had either broadened his choice of victims to delinquents and runaways, or had grown more careful in getting rid of them. "This guy doesn't want to get caught," Bundy told Keppel. "I think it's clear that, over time, you can see him trying to improve his dump sites. He's trying to get better at disposing of those bodies."

Ridgway, it now seems, had done both. The families of several victims have disputed the label of prostitute. Some said their daughters, mothers, sisters, cousins, friends were troubled or just liked to hitchhike.

And apparently Ridgway had a particularly chilling reason to get better at hiding his victims' bodies. Those dead women were his possessions, and he didn't want to lose them. It disturbed him when they were found. He had a recurring dream where he was unable to recall where he left one of "his" bodies and thereby lost control of her.

"I had control of her when I killed her, and I had control over if she hasn't already been found. I'd have control over her where she was still in my possession," he said.

That sense of possession drove him to pin two victims underwater with large rocks. At the time, police had already found an earlier victim.

"I wasn't going to let this other one get away," he said of one of the victims he pinned down in the Green River.

But while the bodies seemed important to him, the women were not. He could not remember faces or races and called many of the victims "it" when telling police details about the killings and dumping the bodies.

Bundy was right about another thing.

"My guess is that he's making his move really quickly, and he's doing it in locations he's very confident in making a move in," Bundy said of how Ridgway likely killed.

Indeed, Ridgway killed many women inside his own bedroom, catching them off-guard immediately after sex and quickly strangling them. He told police that some killings took only minutes. He also quickly disposed of the bodies, usually within half an hour.

Women he didn't kill in his bedroom were murdered in the back of his truck or in the woods in areas Ridgway knew so well that he would take family members to those places for walks or picnics, and wives or girlfriends there for sex.

Bundy studied Ridgway, but Ridgway apparently didn't study Bundy. "I think he was oblivious to Bundy, other than knowing Ted Bundy was someone who had been a serial killer and got caught," Prothero said of Ridgway.

"I don't think he paid much attention to Mr. Bundy's crimes, as far as we can tell."

Ridgway said that during his killing years he didn't read renowned local crime author Ann Rule, either. Rule's first book was about Bundy, and she is now working on a book about Ridgway.

"He read a couple of her books after he was arrested, never before," Prothero said.

∙ ∙ ∙

Researchers call it the "deadly triangle," the three things they see in the backgrounds of killers, especially serial killers: wetting the bed past an appropriate age, setting fires, hurting animals.

Sometimes it's called "the homicidal triangle."

"Research shows that those are red flags, which is fairly consistent across the board with people who have been convicted of violent homicides, sexual homicides," defense attorney Prothero said. "But it isn't 100 percent, and it doesn't mean every bed-wetter is going to turn into a serial killer."

Ridgway had all three of these in his background, he told police.

He wet the bed until age 13. In his pre-adult years, he started a blaze that set a garage on fire. It wasn't the only time. And he once suffocated a cat by putting it in a cooler.

"I don't know that he was ever found out to be responsible for those things," Prothero said, when asked why the deadly triangle was seemingly ignored. "I don't think that people saw the warnings signs and put them together, or cared.

"And the time we're talking about is in the late '50s and early '60s, when the social science on this type of stuff was new. I think we've learned a lot more about those precursors."

It is unclear who knew about other disturbing things Ridgway did when he was younger, especially his stabbing of a 6-year-old boy when Ridgway was 15 or 16. The California man who was stabbed was able to provide prosecutors with details, some of which appear not to have become public at the time of the stabbing, nearly 40 years ago.

Prothero said he believes Ridgway may have been abused as a child, but the killer has said nothing of that, save vivid memories of his mother washing his genitals until he was age 14.

"Maybe he's not wanting to remember things that happened to him in his childhood, his development," Prothero said. "My hunch is that something went terribly wrong there, but he hasn't really been able to disclose anything significant, or any unusually traumatic event from his childhood."

Again, Keppel cautions that none of these things can be corroborated.

Ridgway was a slow learner and a poor reader. As a child, he once paid a child to let him fondle her genitals. He followed girls home while in junior high school and was sexually aroused by it. He acknowledged struggling with the temptation to kill family members, including his wife Judith. He said he rejected the idea because he believed he would get caught. He insists he isn't a rapist, but readily calls himself a murderer. He felt a little remorse, he said, over killing a woman while his child waited nearby in his truck, but then said he likely would've killed his own son if the boy had seen anything.

He tried to blame his second wife for his killing, saying there might have been "a hell of a lot less people dying if I had a nice woman to go home to." He said he was helping police rid the world of prostitutes, whom they couldn't control but he could.

He talked of feeling nothing while killing, but also said it was "painful to see" the face of a 16-year-old he strangled while she was facing him, instead of his usual method of killing his victims from behind. But he quickly discarded that feeling.

"She'd turn me in, and I wouldn't be able to kill anymore. And that meant a lot to me, to kill."

He said he killed his victims quickly and didn't torture any of them or make them feel unnecessary pain.

After acknowledging the things he did — the murderous rampage that never really ended, his hateful thoughts about the people he loved, having sex with bodies even after some of them had decomposed and maggots appeared — he was asked by a detective to rate himself on a scale of one to five, with "five being the worst possible evil person that could have done this kind of thing."

Ridgway's response:

"I'd say a three."

• • •

Keppel, who read the prosecutor's summary, said he thinks

Ridgway is definitely holding out on police.

"What he said about the placing of the rocks in the vaginas of those first river victims? Absolutely phony," Keppel said.

Ridgway told police he placed those rocks because they "were there." But he also alternately "seemed to suggest that he inserted the rocks to 'plug' up his victims." This may be closer to the truth. His second wife had told police that he had "threatened to 'sew up' her vagina to prevent her from having an affair." A triangular-shaped rock was also found in the pelvic area of the skeleton of Constance Naon.

Keppel also said Ridgway gave "half-assed reasons" about posing the body of Carol Christensen, the 21-year-old mother of a 5-year-old daughter. She had two trout placed on her upper torso, an empty Lambrusco wine bottle across her stomach and sausage on her hands.

Ridgway said he used those household items to "throw off" the Task Force. Keppel disagrees.

"He goes into no detail about why he did that. You don't throw the police off doing that," Keppel said. By that time Ridgway had killed more than 20 women. "We don't know how many of the victims were adorned with something," Keppel said. No one except Ridgway knows, because by the time most of their bodies were found, all that remained were skeletons.

"This kind of adornment, it takes a lot of sophisticated, detailed fantasy life, a lot of thinking."

And even though Ridgway has been described as being of average or below average intelligence, Keppel said he disagrees.

"Someone who goes on as long as he did and has as many victims as he did, obviously he has something on the ball. He did get away, but we came awfully close in 1987, and that may be why the long pause in his killing. He's got some intelligence to survive for that long. So you can't take that away from him."

Ridgway took pride in his skills, both in killing and in avoiding detection. He told detectives he was "good in one thing, and that's killing prostitutes."

•••

Ridgway has said he killed more than 60 women, and a tentative list he has made of where he remembers dumping their bodies adds up to 70. For example, Ridgway says he remembers killing up to 11 women and leaving their bodies along Highway 410 near Enumclaw. However, only six have been found there.

Keppel said he doesn't believe Ridgway is leveling with police about how many women he killed. "Ridgway obviously has a lot more murders to talk about some day, under the right circumstances. It could be 60, 70 to 100 altogether."

But getting an accurate final count of how many Ridgway killed may be impossible.

"Many times, with killers, you don't really know what the extent of their murders are," Keppel said. "I think it's going to be troublesome because he's got no way of remembering some of them. Others he's committed, he doesn't want to tell you about.

"For instance, why won't he talk about his last murder? It's probably in a jurisdiction with the death penalty. Or it could be a very special victim for him, and he didn't want to let on that he was the killer of this person."

Ridgway originally told police he last killed in 1985, then changed that to 1990 when confronted with evidence of a case that was similar to the Green River killings. He later changed his story again to say he had killed as recently as 1998.

It could be even later.

"Although he admitted that his last kill was relatively close in time to his arrest in 2001, Ridgway insisted in 2003 that he could recall absolutely nothing about it," prosecutors wrote, adding that Ridgway said he was unable to understand why he would withhold information from police. Then he suggested he remembered the last murder, but didn't want to tell the details "or that the facts were locked away in his head and he could not access them."

Keppel said he thinks there's more to it than that. "They all have secrets they like to hide and keep for their own private fantasy life to have later on in their private moments.

"I think they all know their first victim, but they just don't say," he added.

It could be that police didn't really press Ridgway for information about his first victim, believed to be Wendy Coffield in summer 1982. But prosecutors say that when Ridgway confessed, he insisted he could not remember his first kill. He first claimed it was Coffield, then said that he killed someone several months before her.

And then he admitted that there might have been even

earlier victims.

Ridgway described two or three instances in the 1970s, a decade before the Green River killings "officially" began. He told detectives it was "very possible" he killed women while living in Maple Valley with his second wife. He left the women's bodies in open places, expecting them to be discovered. But when he heard nothing about those "killings," he said he figured the women had regained consciousness and walked away.

"There were others before Coffield that he could've been responsible for," Keppel said. "There were certainly more during the time, and other jurisdictions that have murders that he could quite possibly lay claim to."

•••

Research based on interviews with serial killers has found some characteristics common among them. And Ridgway is in some ways what researchers call a typical serial killer.

He falls into the category of a "stable" killer, as opposed to the "transient" killer. Other stable killers include Gacy.

Stable killers live and work in one location for an extended period, hunt and kill nearby, and dispose of bodies in the same or similar areas. They select hidden disposal sites, may return to the crime scene or burial site and seldom travel (although when they do, it is usually for business, family visits, or personal recreation.)

Ridgway could also be viewed as an organized, rather than disorganized killer.

Most serial killers, about 75 percent of them, are classified by researchers as organized and the victim counts of these killers seem to be higher. Researchers believe that is because they are usually above average intelligence. Bundy and Gacy fall into this group.

An organized killer typically plans out the murder, personalizes himself with the victim (talks, leads or captures the victim into the planned murder situation), rapes or tortures before the murder for his own sexual gratification and kills victims with an awareness of evidence at the crime scene. They may clean bodies or murder scenes and destroy evidence, or plant phony evidence. An organized killer also might move a body to hide or bury it in an attempt to evade or delay its discovery.

But Ridgway is also unlike organized killers. He returned to bodies, and he did not take some item to keep as "trophies" of his kills.

Some serial killers display both disorganized and organized characteristics. Such killers are categorized as being "mixed."

But Ridgway is also a series of contradictions. Keppel said there is no typical serial killer. They're all different, with the exception of liking to kill again and again.

• • •

Prothero said Ridgway calls himself a Christian.

"By all reports there was a time when he was more religious than other times," he said of co-workers' claims that Ridgway often read the Bible at work.

"There's no doubt that he knows the killings were wrong, in a legal sense, a moral sense, a Christian sense. There is no reconciling that. He's tormented by what he's done. He's not happy or proud of it, as it's popular to believe. At least, that is not my sense. I think inside he is very ashamed and tormented."

There aren't concrete answers to the questions about Ridgway — why he killed, what he was thinking. More answers might come after Ridgway is sentenced. Police are still looking for the remains of the victims Ridgway says he remembers killing.

In the meantime, prosecutors have offered this:

"He suffered from no mental illness that could absolve him of responsibility for these crimes. He murdered his victims deliberately, methodically, and systematically. He was uninhibited by any moral concerns. In five months of interviews, he displayed no empathy for his victims and expressed no genuine remorse.

"He killed because he wanted to. He killed because he could. He killed to satisfy his evil and unfathomable desires."

Epilogue

ONE LEGACY OF THE GREEN RIVER INVESTIGATION is that homicide detectives are much better prepared and trained to catch killers.

Many investigators with the King County Sheriff's Office are now considered national experts at processing outdoor crimes scenes and are called on to assist departments across the country.

Another result is the Washington State Attorney General's Homicide Investigation Tracking System — HITS.

HITS keeps a promise that investigator Robert Keppel made when he left the Task Force for the AG's office — to keep track of murders of women and girls in Washington. The system now contains information about every murder in Washington state from 1981 to the present. It provides investigators with instant information about violent crimes such as murder and sexual assault. It tracks missing persons who may be victims of foul play. It sorts through 250 fields of information to match current crimes with similar ones over the past two decades.

The HITS Web site can be accessed at www.atg.wa.gov/hits.

Many of the figures in the Green River investigation have retired, but several remain in law enforcement today.

Dave Reichert

As a young detective, Reichert became the lead investigator in the Green River killings, starting with the murder of Debra Bonner, the second known Green River victim. (Investigation of the first victim, Wendy Coffield, was handled by Kent Police.) Reichert left the case in 1990 and quickly worked his way up through the ranks of the King County Police Department. He was appointed sheriff in 1997 and has been elected to the office since then.

Richard Kraske

Maj. Kraske commanded the Criminal Investigations Division of the King County Police Department, now the King County Sheriff's

Office, in the early 1980s. He made the decisions in the critical first two years of the Green River investigation. He is now retired.

Frank Adamson
Capt. Adamson was commander of the Green River Task Force in 1984-1986. He went on to command the sheriff's Maple Valley precinct and is now retired.

Vern Thomas
Sheriff Thomas was instrumental in getting the money and the political support for the enhanced Green River Task Force that was formed in early 1984. He is now retired.

Robert Keppel
Detective Keppel investigated the Ted Bundy serial murders in the early 1970s for the King County Police Department and as a special investigator for the Washington State Attorney General's Office. He worked closely with the Green River Task Force as a consultant. He now teaches at Sam Houston State University in Texas. He has rewritten and updated his book "The Riverman" to include information about Ridgway.

Jim Montgomery
Sheriff Montgomery oversaw the last two years of the formal Green River investigation after he was appointed sheriff in 1988. He left the county department in 1997 to become the Bellevue police chief.

Bob Evans
Capt. Evans commanded the Task Force in 1988 and 1989 when its investigators and resources were being reassigned to other cases. He is now retired from the Sheriff's Office and has consulted for local TV stations.

Randy Mullinax
Detective Mullinax served on the Green River Task Force for four years starting in 1984. He interviewed Gary Ridgway in April 1984. Later he worked in the major crimes unit and the criminal intelligence unit of the county police department and was assigned to the new Task

Force in 2001. Late that year he and James Doyon arrested Ridgway.

Sue Peters
As a patrol officer, Peters helped detective Dave Reichert process the scene where the bodies of three women were found in August 1982 in Kent. As a detective, she served on the Task Force, then moved on to the major crimes unit. She was named to the new Task Force in 2001.

James Doyon
Detective Doyon joined the Task Force in 1984. He was one of two detectives who interviewed Ridgway's second wife, Marcia, in the 1980s. She gave detectives key insights into Ridgway. He worked on the case until 1991, after which he spent most of his time in the major crimes unit. He was appointed to the new Task Force in 2001, and with Randy Mullinax arrested Ridgway that November.

Tom Jensen
Detective Jensen joined the Task Force in 1984 and never left. In the 1990s, he continued to follow up leads in the Green River investigation as the only detective assigned full-time to the case. In March 2001 he asked the state crime lab to retest the DNA that led to Ridgway's arrest and convictions. He retired in 2002 but was almost immediately asked to work for the new Task Force as a consultant.

Fabienne Brooks
Detective Fabienne Brooks was a spokeswoman and investigator for the Green River investigation for part of the 1980s. She went on to command the sheriff's Maple Valley precinct and is now chief of the Criminal Investigations Division.

Rob Kellams
As a police officer with the Kent Police Department, he investigated the murder of Wendy Coffield. He is a motorcycle police officer for Kent police.

Other figures in the Green River investigations include:
Galen Hirschi and Robert Anderson
As teenagers, Hirschi and Anderson found Wendy Coffield's body

— the first Green River victim — in the Green River in July 1982. Hirschi lives in Auburn and works in information technology for the city of Kent. Anderson lives in Salt Lake City, Utah, and is a computer programmer.

Melvyn Foster

The former cab driver from Lacey was one of the early suspects in the Green River killings. The case haunted him and his family for years. Now retired and still living in the Olympia area, Foster has asked the King County Sheriff's Office to return all of the personal belongings they seized from him during a search in the 1980s.

Matthew Ridgway

Gary Ridgway's adult son is married and lives in the San Diego area. "This is very difficult for him," Ridgway defense attorney Mark Prothero said. "He's doing his best to reconcile and work through this. Gary's probably most remorseful about the pain he's caused his son. But I don't think Gary was close to anyone ever."

Judith Ridgway

Ridgway's third wife is legally separated from him. She visited him regularly until after the second set of charges were filed against her husband in March 2003. She lives in Pierce County under an assumed name. She has declined media interviews.

Timeline

1947

Sept. 1 — First commercial flight at Seattle-Tacoma Airport, which became Seattle-Tacoma International Airport in 1949. Motels, hotels and commercial businesses spring up along Pacific Highway South to serve travelers.

1949

Feb. 18 — Gary Leon Ridgway is born in Salt Lake City to Thomas and Mary Rita Ridgway. He has two brothers, Gregory L. and Thomas E., who are now both in their 50s. According to their father's will, Thomas had another son, Roy Edward Hollowell.

1960

Aug. 16 — Ridgway's family buys a house at 4404 S. 175th St. in McMicken Heights, which is now part of SeaTac.

1962

May 12 — Howard Hanson Dam on the Green River is dedicated, opening the floodgates to development in south King County. The region boomed, with plenty of low-cost housing — and low-paying jobs.

1968

July 31 — Southcenter Shopping Mall opens in Tukwila, becomes another economic engine for South King County.

1969

April 2 — Ridgway is hired as an hourly employee at Kenworth Truck Co., a truck maker in Seattle.

June — Ridgway graduates from Tyee High School at age 20. He also attended Chinook Junior High School and Bow Lake Elementary School in the Highline School District.

Aug. 18 — Ridgway enlists in the U.S. Navy.

December — Ridgway is diagnosed with gonorrhea, according to

Navy medical records.

1970

Aug. 15 — Ridgway marries Claudia Kraig at Fort Lawton Chapel. Claudia is living in San Diego, Calif., while Ridgway completes a six-month sea tour in the Western Pacific.

1971

July 23 — Ridgway is discharged from the Navy. He later returns to work at Kenworth.

1972

Jan. 14 — Ridgway is divorced from Claudia Kraig.

1973

Dec. 14 — Ridgway marries Marcia Lorene Winslow.

1975

Sept. 5 — Matthew, the son of Ridgway and Marcia Winslow, is born.

1977

June 4 — Ridgway buys a maroon 1975 Dodge pickup truck, with numerous rust-colored primer spots.

1980

July 17 — Marcia Ridgway files complaint with Kent Police Department, in which she claims Ridgway is harassing her over the phone about divorce papers. She reports Ridgway is going to get a gun and blow her boyfriend's head off.

July 20 — The Ridgways get into a physical fight, according to Kent police. Both are said to have "bad tempers."

July 21 — Ridgway is accused of choking a prostitute.

1981

May 1981 — Ridgway meets Nancy Palmer at a Parents Without Partners meeting. Their first sexual contact outdoors is in an Army bunker at Fort Casey on Whidbey Island in Puget Sound. He occasionally ties her up before sex.

May 27 — Ridgway is divorced from Marcia, his second wife.

November or December — Ridgway meets a new girlfriend, Sharon Hebert, through Parents Without Partners. Hebert says Ridgway has low self-esteem and was never able to please his mother with his actions.

December — Palmer asks Ridgway to move out.

Dec. 24 — Ridgway shows up about 11 p.m. at a Parents Without Partners social function at the White Shutters Inn on Pacific Highway South. He seems upset and tells Hebert he nearly killed a woman, perhaps a prostitute.

1982

THE CASE: The first victims are found and the case gets its name — the Green River killings. In August the King County Police Department and other local police agencies launch a major investigation. Speculation grows that a serial killer is at work. Many of the victims have ties to prostitution, drugs and street life and were last seen near what was then called the Sea-Tac Strip, the stretch of Pacific Highway South near Seattle-Tacoma International Airport where there were numerous bars, dance clubs and street life. During 1982, Ridgway is arrested for approaching a police decoy during a prostitution sting. Seventeen women will go missing this year; the remains of six are found.

January 1982 — Gary Ridgway lives at 21859 32nd Place S. in SeaTac, about three miles from where the first victims were found in the Green River in Kent. Many of his victims were killed in this house, where he lives until August 1989.

January — Ridgway meets a future girlfriend, Roxanne Theno, at Parents Without Partners dance in Normandy Park.

Feb. 18 — Ridgway turns 33.

April — A husband and wife move into Ridgway's SeaTac house to help pay his bills. Ridgway lives in the garage that has been converted into a living area. The woman says he is rarely at home at night.

May 11 — Ridgway is arrested for agreeing to an act of sex for money with an undercover King County police officer. He is driving a maroon-colored 1975 Dodge pickup truck.

May or June — Hebert breaks off relationship, after Theno tells her Ridgway gave her herpes.

July 7 — Amina Agisheff, 36, is last seen leaving a Seattle apartment. Ridgway is a suspect in her death but has not been charged.

July 8 — Wendy Lee Coffield, 16, is last seen in Tacoma.

July 15 — Coffield's body is found in the Green River in Kent just north of the bridge on Meeker Street.

July 17 — Gisele Ann Lovvorn, 17, is last seen near Sea-Tac Airport.

July 19 — Detectives knock on Virginia Coffield's door in Enumclaw to tell her that her daughter Wendy is dead.

July 25 — Debra Lynn Bonner, 23, is last seen south of Sea-Tac Airport leaving a motel.

Aug. 1 — Marcia Chapman, 31, is last seen headed for the Sea-Tac Strip.

Aug. 11 — Cynthia Jean Hinds, 17, is last seen near the Strip.

Aug. 12 — Opal Charmaine Mills, 16, is last seen at a public phone booth off the Strip. Debra Lynn Bonner's body is found in the Green River in Kent. Detective Dave Reichert joins the investigation.

Aug. 15 — The bodies of Marcia Chapman, Cynthia Hinds and Opal Mills are found in or near the Green River near Kent.

Aug. 27 — Opal Mills is buried. Her minister warns that "young people today must watch out for their environment."

Aug. 28 — Kase Ann Lee, 16, is last seen at 11:30 a.m. at her south King County home by her husband. Her remains haven't been found. Ridgway is a suspect in her death but has not been charged.

Aug. 29 — Ridgway is contacted by Port of Seattle police in his 1975 Dodge pickup truck at 1:14 a.m. at South 192nd Street, near the old Alaska Airlines maintenance building. Later the remains of three Green River victims are found in the area.

Aug. 29 — Terry Rene Milligan, 16, is last seen on the Strip near South 144th Street.

Sept. 9 — Melvyn Foster of Lacey offers to help investigate the murders and immediately raises detectives' suspicions.

Sept. 15 — Mary Bridget Meehan, 18, is last seen on the Strip near a motel. She is seven months pregnant.

Sept. 20 — Debra Lorraine Estes, 15, is last seen at South 333rd Street and Pacific Highway South near a motel.

Sept. 25 — The remains of Gisele Lovvorn are found near an apple tree in Des Moines Creek Park near South 200th Street and

18th Avenue South, south of the airport.

Sept. 26 — Linda Jane Rule, 16, is last seen in mid-afternoon on Aurora Avenue in north Seattle.

October — The renters move from Ridgway's SeaTac home.

Oct. 8 — Denise Darcel Bush, 23, is last seen around noon on the Strip leaving a motel.

Early October — Shawnda Leea Summers, 17, is last seen on the Strip.

Oct. 15 — Task Force identifies another possible suspect, 35-year-old John Norris Hanks, who is jailed in California. He also was tied to strangulations in San Francisco.

Oct. 20-22 — Shirley Marie Sherrill, 18, is last seen in Seattle's International District.

Nov. 9 — Rebecca Garde Guay says she is violently assaulted by a man she later identifies as Ridgway during a "date" near South 204th Street just off Pacific Highway South. She denies she bit him during oral sex, as he claims. He chokes her, but she escapes. She doesn't report the attack for two years.

Dec. 3 — Rebecca T. Marrero, 20, is last seen at Western Six Motel on the Strip. Her remains haven't been found.

Dec. 24 — Colleen Renee Brockman, 15, is last seen in downtown Seattle.

1983

THE CASE: Twenty-seven young women disappear, the most in any one year. The remains of nine women are found through the year near Sea-Tac Airport, near Mountain View Cemetery in Auburn, in Maple Valley, near Auburn-Black Diamond Road and elsewhere.

Jan. 25 — John Norris Hanks is no longer a suspect after he passes a lie-detector test.

Jan. 31 — The remains of Linda Rule are found by construction workers in a wooded area near Northwest Hospital in North Seattle.

Feb. 23 — Ridgway has a "date" with Keli McGinness at South 140th Street and 22nd Avenue South in his 1975 Dodge pickup. It is interrupted by a Port of Seattle police officer.

March-May — Ridgway borrows his brother's blue-green 1970 Dodge pickup truck and his father's 1978 brown and tan pickup truck while he installs a V-8 engine in his maroon

Dodge pickup.

March 3 — Alma Anne Smith, 18, is last seen on the Strip by a friend and prostitute. The friend briefly talks with a man in a white and blue pickup truck; about 3½ years later, looking at a photo montage, she picks Ridgway as looking like the man. She can't positively identify him, however.

March 8-17 — Delores LaVerne Williams, 17, is last seen at a bus stop on the Strip.

April 10 — Gail Lynn Mathews, 23, is last seen by her boyfriend at South 216th Street and Pacific Highway South. He leaves the tavern to go gambling, but sees her in a blue and green pickup truck.

April 14 — Andrea M. Childers, 19, is last seen at a bus stop in Seattle. She apparently was headed for Southcenter.

April 17 — Sandra K Gabbert, 17, is last seen on the Strip.

April 17 — Kimi-Kai Pitsor, 16, is last seen in Seattle by her boyfriend.

April 30 — Marie M. Malvar, 18, is last seen near South 216th Street and Pacific Highway South by her pimp. She gets into a dark-colored pickup truck.

May 3 — Carol Ann Christensen, 21, is last seen at the Barn Door Tavern on Pacific Highway South in SeaTac where she works.

May 4 — Malvar's pimp contacts detective with the Des Moines Police Department to report he has found the truck associated with her disappearance. The detective interviews Ridgway at his home at 21859 32nd Place S. in SeaTac. He denies any involvement in her disappearance. It's the first time Ridgway comes to the attention of the Green River Task Force. Marie Malvar's father, Jose, also contacts Des Moines police.

May 8 — The remains of Carol Christensen are found in a wooded area of Maple Valley. Her body is posed with trout, wine bottle and sausage.

May 22 — Martina Theresa Authorlee, 18, is last seen at a motel on the Strip.

May 23 — Cheryl Lee Wims, 18, is last seen in Seattle.

May 31 — Yvonne Shelly Antosh, 19, is last seen on the Strip.

May 31-June 15 — Carrie Rois disappears, but the circumstances are unknown. She had been arrested for prostitution on the Strip. At 15, she was one of the youngest victims.

June 8 — Constance Elizabeth Naon, 20, is last seen on the Strip.

June 9 — Tammie Charlene Liles, 16, is last seen in downtown

Seattle. Ridgway is a suspect in her death but has not been charged.

June 28 — Keli K. McGinness, 18, is last seen on the Strip. Her remains have never been found. Ridgway is a suspect in her death but has not been charged.

July 18 — Kelly Marie Ware, 22, is last seen at a Seattle bus stop.

July 25 — Tina Marie Thompson, 22, is last seen at a motel on the Strip.

Aug. 11 — The remains of Shawnda Leea Summers are found at the base of an apple tree north of Sea-Tac Airport near South 146th Street and 16th Avenue South.

Aug. 18-Sept. 1 — April Dawn Buttram, 17, is last seen in the 7300 block of Rainier Avenue South in Seattle.

Sept. 5 — Debbie May Abernathy, 26, is last seen when she leaves her apartment near Rainier Avenue to go to downtown Seattle.

Sept. 12 — Tracy Ann Winston, 19, is last seen at Seattle's Northgate Mall.

Sept. 18 — The remains of Gail Lynn Mathews are found at the base of a fir tree near Star Lake Road near 55th Avenue South and South 272nd Street in Auburn.

Sept. 28 — Maureen Sue Feeney, 19, is last seen at a Seattle bus stop.

Oct. 11 — Mary Sue Bello, 25, is last seen in downtown Seattle.

Oct. 15 — The remains of Yvonne Antosh are found near Soos Creek in Auburn.

Oct. 20 — Patricia Anne Osborn, 19, is last seen in the 11500 block of Aurora Avenue North in Seattle. Her remains have not been found. Ridgway is a suspect in her death but hasn't been charged.

Oct. 26 — Pammy Avent, 16, is last seen about 7:30 p.m. at her mother's home in South Seattle.

Oct. 27 — The remains of Constance Naon are found near the 2500 block of South 192nd Street just south of Sea-Tac Airport.

Oct. 29 — The remains of Kelly Marie Ware are found near the 2500 block of South 192nd Street just south of Sea-Tac Airport.

Oct. 30 — Delise Louise Plager, 22, is last seen at a bus stop on Beacon Hill in Seattle.

Late October — Ridgway starts working 3:40 p.m. to 12:10 a.m. at Kenworth.

Nov. 1 — Kimberly L. Nelson, 20, is last seen at bus stop at South 144th Street and Pacific Highway South by a fellow prostitute. The man she left with is white, late 20s to early 30s, with brown hair and a wispy mustache. Nelson's friend later identifies Ridgway from a photo montage.

Nov. 13 — The remains of Mary Bridget Meehan are found partially buried near South 192nd Street and 27th Avenue South, just south of Sea-Tac Airport.

Nov. 16 — Ridgway is interviewed by Green River Task Force detective Larry Gross.

Dec. 15 — The skull of Kimi-Kai Pitsor is found near Mountain View Cemetery in Auburn. Other remains are found there December 1985.

Dec. 23 — Lisa Yates, 19, is last seen in South Seattle.

1984

THE CASE: The number of victims found rises to 14 as a "cluster" of four is found on Auburn's West Hill near Star Lake Road. Other remains are found east of Enumclaw and near Sumner in Pierce County. The enhanced Green River Task Force is formed.

January — The Green River Task Force is made official and expanded to 36 full-time investigators.

Feb. 3 — A prostitute contacts the Task Force to report Ridgway as a suspect. Detective Randy Mullinax investigates.

Feb. 6 — Mary Exzetta West, 16, is last seen in South Seattle.

Feb. 14 — The remains of Delise Plager are found near Exit 38 off Interstate 90 east of North Bend.

Feb. 21 — Ridgway's maroon 1975 Dodge pickup truck is totaled in an accident.

March 13 — The remains of Lisa Yates are found near Exit 38 off Interstate 90 east of North Bend. Cindy Anne Smith, 17, is last seen hitchhiking on Pacific Highway South. For nearly 20 years, she is presumed to be the Green River killer's last victim.

March 21 — Remains are found north of Sea-Tac Airport near baseball field. They are still unidentified.

March 22 — The remains of Cheryl Lee Wims are found just north of Sea-Tac Airport.

March 31 — The remains of Delores LaVerne Williams are found near Star Lake Road. The remains of Debbie May Abernathy are found about a dozen miles east of Enumclaw near a logging road.

April 1 — The remains of Terry Rene Milligan are found near Star Lake Road. The remains of Sandra K Gabbert are found near Star Lake Road.

April 2 — The remains of Alma Anne Smith are found near Star Lake Road.

April 12 — Detective Randy Mullinax interviews Ridgway, who describes a "date" with Keli McGinness and seeing or contacting numerous prostitutes on Pacific Highway South, including victim Kim Nelson.

April 18 — The remains of Amina Agisheff found near Highway 18 and Interstate 90, nearly two years after her disappearance.

April 20 — The remains of Tina Marie Thompson are found near Highway 18 and Interstate 90 by Kent psychic Barbara Kubik-Patten, who alerts detectives searching about a mile away.

May 7 — Ridgway passes a polygraph examination. Coupled with a follow-up investigation, "Ridgway was considered to be cleared as a possible Green River suspect," according to court documents. A later examination of the polygraph results by two experts showed that the exam was incomplete and therefore invalid.

May 26 — The remains of Colleen Renee Brockman are found near Sumner in Pierce County.

June — Ridgway and Roxanne Theno plan to get married, but she calls it off after meeting someone else.

June — Task Force gets a $200,000 computer to index, file and retrieve evidence collected in the case.

Oct. 12 — The remains of Mary Sue Bello are found eight miles east of Enumclaw on Highway 410.

Nov. 8 — Capt. Frank Adamson, head of the Task Force, says it would be a mistake to say the killings have stopped, even though it has been almost a year since the last known victim was murdered.

Nov. 14 — The remains of Martina Theresa Authorlee are found east of Enumclaw.

Nov. 29 — Prostitute Rebecca Garde Guay calls Task Force to report she was violently assaulted while working as a prostitute in November 1982. An investigation leads detectives to Ridgway as the attacker.

1985

THE CASE: Many people simply can't believe the Green River Task Force is unable to track down the killer. More detectives join the effort. Ridgway's file is reopened by the Task Force after a prostitute reported he tried to kill her on Nov. 9, 1982. Ridgway file turned over to two FBI special agents. The agents interview Ridgway several months later.

Feb. 23 — Ridgway admits to Task Force detective he choked Rebecca Garde Guay in 1982 after paying for a sex act during which he says she bit him. He also admits to "dating" on Aurora Avenue North and in Seattle, and says he probably dated some of the victims.

March 10 — The remains of Carrie A. Rois are found near Star Lake Road in Auburn.

April 23 — The remains of Tammie Charlene Liles are found in Tualatin, Ore., south of Portland.

April 23 — Remains found in Tualatin, Ore.; still unidentified.

June 12 — The skull of Denise Darcel Bush is found in Tigard, Ore., south of Portland. Investigators believe the killer moved part of her remains. Body appears to have been left first in wooded area in Tukwila. Some skeletal remains found there Feb. 10, 1990.

June 14 — The remains of Shirley Marie Sherrill are found in Tigard, near those of Denise Bush.

Sept. 8 — The remains of Mary Exzetta West are found in Seattle's Seward Park.

Nov. 12 — Task Force gets $1 million in federal funds to help solve the Green River killings.

Dec. 31 — Remains found near Auburn's Mountain View Cemetery; still unidentified.

1986

THE CASE: Skeletal remains of four more victims are found. Public pressure grows for an arrest. Task Force detectives become more frustrated as women's advocacy groups and other critics claim the case would be solved if the victims were middle-class college women instead of those linked to the streets. The Task Force grows to 55 investigators, plus support staff. The county invests in new computer systems to handle thousands of possible suspects and thousands of leads.

Feb. 6 — The FBI and the Task Force search the home of a Riverton Heights man — Ernest W. "Bill" McLean — in connection with the murders. Considered a "strong suspect," he is questioned for 11 hours.

March 17 — Ridgway tells FBI agents he has not dated prostitutes in the last year and a half because of the Green River killings and the fact he has caught a venereal disease at least 15 times. Although he has a fixation with prostitutes, he says, during the last year and a half he has picked up prostitutes in his vehicle only to talk to them. He says prostitutes may "affect him as strongly as alcohol does an alcoholic."

March 20 — Ridgway agrees to a second polygraph to be administered by the FBI; but his attorney, David Middaugh, telephones the FBI and says not to contact his client. Ridgway fails to appear for the second polygraph. FBI inactivates the Ridgway investigation.

March 27 — The remains of Tracy Ann Winston are found near the Green River in Kent but not identified until 1999.

May — Bill McLean is cleared, but he still feels he's a prime suspect.

May 2 — The remains of Maureen Sue Feeney are found off Interstate 90 near North Bend.

June 14 — The remains of Kimberly L. Nelson are found on Garcia Road near Exit 38 off Interstate 90 near North Bend.

July — A university study finds that the Green River serial murder case was one of the 25 stories most overlooked by the national media in 1985. The lead professor says that editors and reporters ignored the case out of personal bias because many of the victims were prostitutes, some of them black.

July 15 — Members of a group calling itself the Women's Coalition to Stop the Green River Murders picket and chain themselves to the door of the Task Force headquarters in the King County Courthouse, demanding more be done.

Aug. 12 — Task Force interviews a prostitute, Paige Miley, who provides them with key details about the disappearance of Kimberly Nelson, including identifying Ridgway as possibly her last "date."

Aug. 19 — Ridgway case is reopened by Task Force detectives who have reviewed the file and determined there are still unresolved questions.

Sept. 14 — Ridgway's ex-wife, Marcia, shows Task Force detectives several areas where they went, often for sex, during their relationship. These include Highway 18 and Interstate 90, the middle fork of the Snoqualmie River near North Bend, the Greenwater area near Enumclaw and Star Lake near Kent where the remains of six victims were found.

Sept. 18 — Twelve members of the Task Force are reassigned to other duties. It will have 20 officers when the reassignments are completed. The Task Force has a $2 million budget.

Oct. 9-24 — Ridgway is surveilled in the morning and afternoon before he starts work at the Kenworth Truck Co. plant on East Marginal Way in Seattle at 3:40 p.m. He also occasionally is watched after leaving work at 12:10 a.m. He is seen cruising and parking along Pacific Highway South. Once he goes to an area along Rainier Avenue South from which four Green River victims disappeared, including April Buttram.

Oct. 17 — Patricia Michelle Barczak, 19, is last seen near the Airporter Motel on the Strip.

December — Task Force made aware of the remains of two women found in wooded areas northeast of Vancouver, British Columbia.

1987

THE CASE: Washington State Patrol Crime Lab can't link Ridgway to any of the Green River killings with evidence taken from him, his house and his vehicles.

January — After looking at photo montages, boyfriend of victim Kimi-Kai Pitsor "can't be a thousand percent sure" she got into a truck driven by Ridgway.

Feb. 7 — Roberta Hayes, 21, is last seen after she is released from the Portland, Ore., jail after an arrest for prostitution.

April 8 — Ridgway plucks hair from his head, chest and pubic area for investigators after search warrant is issued. He also gives a saliva sample. Also searched are his home, three vehicles he has used and his personal locker at the Kenworth plant in Seattle.

April 8 — Detectives interview Ridgway's brother, Thomas, who reports that in mid-1986 Ridgway replaced the carpets in his house.

May — Prostitutes are returning to the Strip as fear of the killer fades.

June 27 — The remains of Cindy Anne Smith are found off Highway 18 near Green River Community College.

1988

THE CASE: Ridgway marries a third wife, Judith Lynch, and the Task Force turns to a national TV audience in hopes of getting clues that will solve the case.

May 30 — The remains of Debra Lorraine Estes are found by construction workers at South 348th Street and First Avenue South in Federal Way. She disappeared about 5 1/2 years ago.
June 12 — Ridgway, then 38, and 43-year-old Judith Lynch are married at 2 p.m. in a neighbor's yard.
August — Task Force members go to San Diego, Calif., to investigate possible links between the Green River case and 34 murders there.
December — The bill to operate the Task Force investigating the killings reaches about $13 million.
Dec. 7 — A two-hour special, "Manhunt ... Live: A Chance to End the Nightmare" is broadcast nationwide, offering a $100,000 reward for information leading to arrest of the Green River killer. The show generates 16,000 calls and 1,500 potential leads — but no immediate arrests.

1989

THE CASE: Gary Ridgway and his wife, Judith, move to Des Moines. A suspect is arrested but later cleared.

Jan. 9 — A 38-year-old Gonzaga University student, William J. Stevens II, is jailed as a possible suspect in the Green River killings. The tip came from the "Manhunt ... Live" program. He was never charged.
September — Gary Ridgway moves to 2139 S. 253rd St. in Des Moines, where he lives until November 1997.
Oct. 11 — The remains of Andrea M. Childers are found in a shallow grave in a wooded area south of Sea-Tac Airport.

The 1990s

THE CASE: With an apparent end to the killings, some speculate the killer is in jail, has died or has left the area. But women continue to disappear throughout the Northwest. The Green River Task Force is gradually reduced, until only one detective continues to field tips and check out potential leads.

Feb. 28, 1990 — The city of SeaTac incorporates, partly in response to the decades of prostitution along the notorious Sea-Tac Strip that runs through the city's heart. SeaTac City Council adopts a Stay Out of Areas of Prostitution ordinance, which calls for enhanced fines for soliciting prostitutes in designated areas such as Pacific Highway South.

March 5 or 6, 1990 — Marta Reeves, 36, has her last contact with her estranged husband. She spent much time in the Seattle Central area.

April 1, 1990 — Dave Reichert leaves the Task Force when he is promoted to sergeant. He commands the patrolmen on the graveyard shift at the Burien precinct, which includes the Strip.

April 10, 1990 — In an interview, Reichert, once the lead investigator in the Green River killings, admits that during the investigation he became so obsessed with solving the case that his personality changed. He became aloof and he ignored his family. But he still expects to find the killer.

May 12, 1990 — Ridgway reports to Kent police that a box of distributor caps and rotors was stolen from his booth at the Midway swap meet on Pacific Highway South.

Sept. 20, 1990 — The remains of Marta Reeves are found by mushroom hunters just off Highway 410 east of Enumclaw.

Sept. 11, 1991 — The remains of Roberta Hayes are found at the end of a dirt road north of Highway 410 and east of Enumclaw

Nov. 5, 1991 — The remains of Sarah Habakangas are found off Interstate 90 near Exit 38. She had ties either to prostitution or street life but isn't added to the Green River list.

July 15, 1992 — It has been 10 years since the body of Wendy Coffield was found. The best chance to catch the killer or killers may have passed. The Task Force has a size $10_{1/2}$ shoe print, a number of pickup truck sightings and four composite photos of white men.

Nov. 7, 1992 — The remains of Nicole French are found in the North Bend area. She also has ties either to prostitution or street life, but isn't added to the Green River list.

February 1993 — Patricia Barczak's remains are found off Highway 18 near Seattle International Raceway.

November 1997 — Reichert is elected King County sheriff. Gary and Judith Ridgway move to a home in Auburn.

Jan. 21, 1998 — Ridgway's father, Thomas, a retired Metro bus driver, dies of pneumonia. A contributing cause was dementia. He was 74.

Aug. 6, 1998 — The body of Patricia Yellowrobe is found in South Park near a wrecking yard. Her death is ruled a drug overdose.

Nov. 3, 1999 — One of five sets of skeletal remains is identified by DNA testing as Tracy Ann Winston, whose remains were found in 1986.

2001

THE CASE: DNA test results in September link Ridgway to three of the Green River victims — Opal Mills, Marcia Chapman and Carol Christensen. Results positively clear two other longtime suspects in the case. Police keep Ridgway under close surveillance. Then comes the arrest.

Feb. 18 — Ridgway turns 52.

Aug. 15 — Ridgway's 73-year-old mother, Mary Rita, dies.

September — DNA tests conducted by the Washington State Patrol Crime Lab connect Ridgway to three victims.

Sept. 11 — Sheriff Dave Reichert asks Capt. Jim Graddon, who patrolled the strip 25 years ago, to head up an "evidence review team" that would operate "under the radar." Two days later, Graddon learns their target. It is Ridgway. Graddon says it was the best-kept secret in law enforcement.

Oct. 17 — Ridgway is watched as he travels the least direct route from his job in Renton to his home in Auburn, along Pacific Highway South. He travels below the speed limit and appears distracted by a woman possibly working as a prostitute.

Oct. 23 — Detectives watch Ridgway after work as he takes Pacific Highway South to his home in Auburn. He makes two unexplainable U-turns in the middle of the highway and stops to visit his mother's house in SeaTac.

Nov. 16 — Ridgway is arrested in SeaTac for loitering for the purpose of prostitution in the 16500 block of Pacific Highway South. He is booked into the King County Jail and is later fined $700.

Nov. 28 — Under watch again, Ridgway leaves his Auburn home at 4:20 a.m., taking an indirect route on Pacific Highway South to his Renton job. A commute of 20 minutes takes an hour. He arrives 45 minutes early for his job.

Nov. 30 — Ridgway is arrested as a suspect in four of the Green River killings as he leaves his job of 30 years at the Kenworth Truck Co. plant in Renton.

Nov. 30-early December — Ridgway's present home on Auburn's West Hill and his previous residences are searched, along with his vehicles and his work locker.

Dec. 5 — Ridgway is charged with four counts of aggravated first-degree murder for the deaths of Marcia Chapman, Cynthia Hinds, Opal Mills and Carol Ann Christensen. Of the four, Hinds is the only one not linked to Ridgway through DNA.

Dec. 8 — Ridgway hires Anthony Savage, one of the state's premier defense attorneys, to defend him.

Dec. 17 — Ridgway's defense team, which now includes public defenders, gets $1 million for in public money for 2002.

Dec. 18 — Ridgway pleads innocent to murder charges; prosecutor yet to decide whether to seek the death penalty.

2002

THE CASE: Detectives try to track down the numerous vehicles Ridgway had access to during the past two decades. Workers busy burning thousands of pages of evidence and tips onto computer discs. Detectives continue to build case and lawyers continue to argue in court.

March 28 — King County Superior Court Judge Richard Jones is picked to hear Ridgway case.

April 12 — Judge Jones agrees to appoint special master to oversee costs of the Ridgway trial.

April 15 — Prosecutor Norm Maleng announces he'll seek the death penalty against Ridgway, if he is found guilty.

Sept. 5 — Ridgway files for divorce from his third wife, Judith.

2003

THE CASE: The new Green River Task Force searches about two dozen sites throughout the county, looking for remains of victims. Four sets of remains are found, including three of suspected victims of the Green River killer. Ridgway strikes a deal.

March 27 — Ridgway is charged with aggravated first-degree murder in the deaths of three more Green River victims, Wendy Coffield, Debra Estes and Debra Bonner.

April 11 — Ridgway admits to his attorneys that he is the Green River killer and enters into plea negotiations with prosecutors that will spare him his life in exchange for cooperating with investigators.

June 13 — Ridgway is released from the ultra-security unit of the county jail in downtown Seattle to the Sheriff's Office. For the next five months, he is held at the Task Force headquarters at Boeing Field where is questioned intensely. He leads investigators to places where he dumped his victims.

Aug. 16 — The remains of Pammy Avent are found off Highway 410 near Enumclaw, nearly 20 years after her disappearance. Ridgway led detectives directly to her body.

Aug. 30 and Sept. 2 — The remains of April Dawn Buttram are found near Snoqualmie just off Interstate 90, 20 years after her disappearance.

Sept. 28 and 29 — The remains of Marie Malvar are found in a steep ravine on Auburn's West Hill.

Nov. 5 — Ridgway pleads guilty to the murders of 48 women; 42 are on the official list of Green River victims, six are not. Four of the women remain unidentified.

Sources: Court documents, police reports and Journal archives.

The Victims

Wendy Lee Coffield, 16

Last seen July 8, 1982, leaving her foster home in Tacoma. Remains found in the Green River in Kent on July 15, 1982.

Gisele Ann Lovvorn, 17

Last seen July 17, 1982, leaving apartment for Pacific Highway South, (Sea-Tac Strip.) Remains found south of airport on Sept. 25, 1982.

Debra Lynn Bonner, 23

Last seen July 25, 1982, leaving a motel on the Strip. Remains found in the Green River in Kent on Aug. 12, 1982.

Marcia Faye Chapman, 31

Last seen Aug. 1, 1982, leaving her apartment near the Strip. Remains found Aug. 15, 1982, in the Green River in Kent.

Cynthia Jean Hinds, 17

Last seen Aug. 11, 1982, on the Strip. Remains found Aug. 15, 1982, in the Green River in Kent.

Opal Charmaine Mills, 16

Last seen Aug. 12, 1982, at a phone booth off the Strip. Remains found Aug. 15, 1982, next to the Green River in Kent.

Terry Rene Milligan, 16

Last seen Aug. 29, 1982, on the Strip. Remains found April 1, 1984, near Star Lake Road between Kent and Auburn.

Mary Bridget Meehan, 18

Last seen Sept. 15, 1982, near a motel on the Strip. Remains found Nov. 13, 1983, south of Sea-Tac Airport.

Debra Lorraine Estes, 15

Last seen Sept. 20, 1982, near a motel on the Strip. Remains found May 30, 1988, in Federal Way.

Linda Jane Rule, 16

Last seen Sept. 26, 1982, on Aurora Avenue in North Seattle. Remains found Jan. 31, 1983, near Northwest Hospital in North Seattle.

Denise Darcel Bush, 23

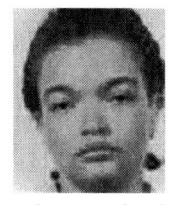

Last seen Oct. 8, 1982, leaving a motel on the Strip. Remains found June 12, 1985, in Tigard, Ore., and on Feb. 10, 1990, in Tukwila.

ShawndaLeea Summers, 17

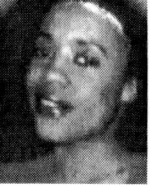

Last seen early October 1982; she was known to work as a prostitute on the Strip. Remains found Aug. 11, 1983, north of Sea-Tac.

Shirley Marie Sherrill, 18

Last seen Oct. 20-22, 1982, in the International District in Seattle. Remains found June 14, 1985, in Tigard, Ore.

Colleen Renee Brockman, 15

Last seen Dec. 24, 1982, at a downtown Seattle motel. Remains found May 26, 1984, near Sumner, Pierce County.

Alma Anne Smith, 18

Last seen March 3, 1983, on the Strip. Remains found April 2, 1984, near Star Lake Road.

Delores LaVerne Williams, 17	**Gail Lynn Mathews, 23**	**Andrea M. Childers, 19**	**Sandra K Gabbert, 17**	**Kimi-Kai Pitsor, 16**	
Last seen between March 8 and 17, 1983, near bus stop on the Strip. Remains found March 31, 1984, near Star Lake Road.	Last seen April 10, 1983, on the Strip. Remains found Sept. 18, 1983, near Star Lake Road.	Last seen April 14, 1983, at a bus stop in Seattle. Remains found Oct. 11, 1989, south of Sea-Tac Airport.	Last seen April 17, 1983, on the Strip. Remains found April 1, 1984, near Star Lake Road.	Last seen April 17, 1983, in downtown Seattle. Skull found Dec. 15, 1983, near Mountain View Cemetery in Auburn. Other remains found there in December 1985.	

Marie M. Malvar, 18	**Carol Ann Christensen, 21**	**Martina Theresa Authorlee, 18**	**Cheryl Lee Wims, 18**	**Yvonne Shelly Antosh, 19**
Last seen April 30, 1983, at a store on the Strip. Remains found Sept. 28 and 29, 2003, near Auburn.	Last seen May 3, 1983, at a tavern on the Strip where she worked. Remains found May 8, 1983, in Maple Valley.	Last seen May 22, 1983, at a motel on the Strip. Remains found Nov. 14, 1984, near Enumclaw.	Last seen May 23, 1983, in Seattle. Remains found March 22, 1984, north of Sea-Tac Airport.	Last seen May 31, 1983, on the Strip. Remains found Oct. 15, 1983, near Soos Creek near Auburn.

Carrie A. Rois, 15	**Constance Elizabeth Naon, 20**	**Kelly Marie Ware, 22**	**Tina Marie Thompson, 22**	**April Dawn Buttram, 17**
Last seen between May 31 and June 15, 1983; the circumstances of her disappearance are not known. Remains found March 10, 1985, near Star Lake Road.	Last seen June 8, 1983, on the Strip. Remains found Oct. 27, 1983, south of Sea-Tac Airport.	Last seen July 18, 1983, in Seattle. Remains found Oct. 29, 1983, south of Sea-Tac Airport.	Last seen July 25, 1983, at a motel on the Strip. Remains found April 20, 1984, near Highway 18 and Interstate 90.	Last seen between Aug. 18 and Sept. 1, 1983, by police on Rainier Avenue. Remains found Aug. 30 and Sept. 2, 2003, in a forested area near Snoqualmie.

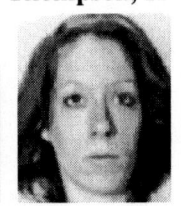

Gary Ridgway: The Green River Killer

Debbie May Abernathy, 26

Last seen Sept. 5, 1983, as she left her apartment near Rainier Avenue to go to downtown Seattle. Remains found March 31, 1984, east of Enumclaw.

Tracy Ann Winston, 19

Last seen Sept. 12, 1983, at Northgate Mall in North Seattle. Remains found March 27, 1986, near the Green River in Kent.

Maureen Sue Feeney, 19

Last seen Sept. 28, 1983, at a Seattle bus stop. Remains found May 2, 1986, off Interstate 90 near North Bend.

Mary Sue Bello, 25

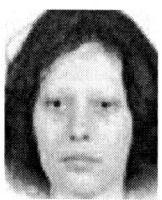

Last seen Oct. 11, 1983, in downtown Seattle. Remains found Oct. 12, 1984, east of Enumclaw.

Pammy Avent, 16

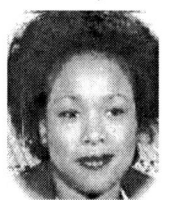

Last seen Oct. 26, 1983, in Seattle. Remains found Aug. 16, 2003, off Highway 410 near Enumclaw.

Delise Louise Plager, 22

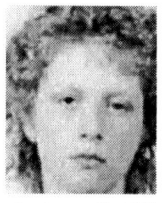

Last seen Oct. 30, 1983, at a bus stop on Seattle's Beacon Hill. Remains found Feb. 14, 1984, near I-90 east of North Bend.

Kimberly L. Nelson, 20

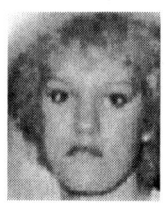

Last seen Nov. 1, 1983, at a bus stop on the Strip. Remains found June 14, 1986, off Interstate 90 near North Bend.

Lisa Yates, 19

Last seen Dec. 23, 1983, on Rainier Avenue in South Seattle. Remains found March 13, 1984, off I-90 east of North Bend.

Mary Exzetta West, 16

Last seen Feb. 6, 1984, on Rainier Avenue in South Seattle. Remains found Sept. 8, 1985, in Seattle's Seward Park.

Cindy Anne Smith, 17

Last seen March 13, 1984, hitchhiking on the Strip. Remains found June 27, 1987, near Green River Community College.

Patricia Michelle Barczak, 19

Last seen Oct. 17, 1986, on the Strip near Sea-Tac. Remains found in February 1993 off Highway 18 near Seattle International Raceway.

Roberta Joseph Hayes, 21

Last seen Feb. 7, 1987, leaving a Portland, Ore., jail. Remains found Sept. 11, 1991, along Highway 410 east of Enumclaw.

Marta Reeves, 36

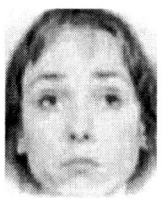

Last heard from March 5 or 6, 1990 when she called her estranged husband for money. Remains found Sept. 20, 1990, along Highway 410 east of Enumclaw.

Patricia Yellowrobe, 38

Body found Aug. 6, 1998, outside the fenced yard of a wrecking yard in South Park. Her death initially ruled a drug overdose.

Jane Doe B-10, found March 21, 1984. May have died as early as Jan. 1, 1982.

Jane Doe B-16, found Dec. 31, 1985. May have died as early as Dec. 1, 1982.

Jane Doe B-17, found Jan. 2, 1986. May have died as early as Dec. 1, 1982.

Jane Doe B-20, bone fragment found Aug. 31, 2003. May have died as early as the mid 1970s.

Index

Abernathy, Debbie 9, 155, 191, 192, 205
Adamson, Frank 65, 70, 73, 75, 79, 80, 81, 106, 113, 182, 193
Agisheff, Amina 9, 155, 163, 173, 188, 193
Anderson, Robert 11, 183, 184
Antosh, Yvonne 9, 190, 191, 204
Armstrong, Thomas Blake 68
Atchley, Frank 103
Authorlee, Martina 9, 190, 193, 204
Avent, Pammy 9, 201, 205

Baird, Jeff 136, 146, 155
Barber, Mike 72
Barczak, Patricia 9, 157, 160, 196, 199, 205
Bello, Mary 9, 191, 193, 205
Bennecke, Shari 87
Blaney, Linda 22
Bonner, Debra 9, 59, 68, 83, 181, 188, 201, 203
Bourne, Randy 37, 83
Brockman, Barry 77
Brockman, Colleen 9, 77, 189, 203
Brooks, Fae 45, 91, 183
Bundy, Ted 63, 117-9, 138, 167, 170-5, 179, 182
Bush, Denise 9, 47, 93, 189, 194, 203
Buttram, April 9, 191, 201, 204

Casanova, Jeanne 17

Chapman, Marcia 9, 18, 50, 59, 63, 122, 123, 128, 188, 199, 200, 203
Childers, Andrea 9, 190, 197, 204
Christensen, Carol 9, 57, 122, 123, 128, 156, 159, 177, 190, 199, 200, 204
Christensen, Sarah 156, 159
Coffield, Virginia 12, 52, 188
Coffield, Wendy 9, 11, 37, 52, 59, 68, 79, 83, 140, 145, 178, 179, 188, 198, 201, 203
Cross, Sandra 50

Davenport, James 69, 70
Davis, Jimmy 19
Dexter, Helen 161
Doll, Mike 87
Douglas, John 71
Doyon, James 61, 74, 93, 115, 117, 128, 182, 183
Du Fresne, Beverly 116
Duffy, Patrick 110
Dyer, David Shawn 70

Eakes, Patricia 136, 139
Eldridge, Keith 91
Estes, Carol 158, 160
Estes, Debra 9, 158, 160, 197, 201, 203
Evans, Gov. Dan 63
Evans, Robert 109, 115

Feeney, Maureen 9, 53, 191, 195, 205

Forsman, Ellis 108
Foster, Melvyn 69, 124, 184, 188
Fox, Robert 57, 66
Fries, Rosemary 157

Gabbert, Nancy 162
Gabbert, Sandra 9, 85, 162, 190, 193, 204
Gacy, John 167, 179
Gehrke, Randy 63
Gies, Rick 45
Girard, Greg 128
Goodhew, Ian 136
Goody, Mary 134
Graddon, Jim 122, 123, 199
Graham, Virginia 158
Gregurek, Clem 116
Griffin, Deniece 52, 101
Gruenhagen, Todd 133, 134
Guay, Rebecca Garde 73, 74, 189, 193, 194
Guillen, Tomas 119

Haglund, Bill 85
Hamamura, Duane 12
Haney, Matthew 106
Hanks, John Norris 69, 124, 189
Hartley, Steve 77
Haven, Bob 29
Hayes, Roberta 9, 196, 198, 205
Hebert, Sharon 27, 28, 29, 187
Hinds, Cynthia 9, 18, 50-2, 59, 63, 101, 124, 128, 188, 200, 203
Hirschi, Galen 11, 12, 183
Hunt, Cookie 78

Jenne, Raymond 80
Jensen, Thomas 61, 93, 99, 115, 117, 120-3, 128, 183
Jones, Richard 62, 132-4, 140, 145, 153-5, 200

Kellams, Rob 37
Keppel, Robert 93, 119, 138, 166-72, 176-82
King County Journal 11, 12, 57
King County Sexual Assault Center 79
Kitching, Al 135
Kraig, Claudia 18, 23, 186
Kraske, Richard 181

Leatherman, Fred 134
Lee, Kase Ann 9, 155, 163, 188
Liles, Tammie 9, 155, 163, 190, 194
Lindell, Eric 134
Lovvorn, Gisele 9, 188, 203

Maleng, Norm 95, 130, 137, 139, 145-7, 153, 154, 200
Malvar, Jose 56-8
Malvar, Marie 9, 46, 55-8, 66, 98, 101, 157, 162, 190, 201, 204
Marrero, Mary 163, 164
Marrero, Perfecto 158, 163
Marrero, Rebecca 9, 155, 158, 163, 189
Mathews, Gail 9, 56, 105, 190, 191, 204
Matthews, Larry Darnell 68
Matzke, Norm 67, 68
McDonald, Brian 136
McGinness, Keli 9, 66, 155, 163, 189, 191, 193
McLean, Ernest W. "Bill" 73, 80, 106, 195

McNeely, Dick 89
McVeigh, Timothy 132
Meehan, Mary 9, 94, 160, 188, 192, 203
Meehan, Tim 94
Middaugh, David 195
Miley, Paige 103-5, 139, 195
Milligan, Terry 9, 85, 188, 193, 203
Mills, Garret 129
Mills, Kathy 49, 51, 119, 157
Mills, Opal 9, 18, 50-2, 60, 63, 101, 119, 122, 123, 128, 129, 138, 157, 188, 199, 200, 203
Mills, Robert 51
Molina, Mary 157, 162
Montgomery, James 62, 117, 182
Mullinax, Randy 61, 65-7, 99, 128, 182, 183, 192

Naon, Constance 9, 155, 161, 190, 191, 204
Nelson, Kimberly 9, 66, 103, 104, 191, 193, 195, 205
Nickals, Golznia 88
Nipertia, Sally 90
Nolan, Dan 90, 110
Nooney, Ross 103

O'Donnell, Sean 136
Ornelas, Cynthia Bassett 105
Osborn, Patricia 9, 163, 191

Palmer, Nancy 28, 29, 187
Patten, Barbara Kubik 64, 86, 193
PD&J Meats 59
Pedrin, Bob 17, 18
Peters, Sue 59, 99, 183

Peterson, Josie 164
Pflaumer, Kate 134
Pitsor, Kimi-Kai 9, 162, 190, 192, 196, 204
Plager, Delise 9, 191, 192, 205
Plemons, Richard 68
Prothero, Mark 128, 133, 134, 136, 144-8, 153, 154, 166, 170, 174-6, 180

Reeves, Marta 9, 115, 119, 198, 205
Reichert, Dave 45, 59, 60-2, 67, 83, 100, 111, 112, 117, 121-3, 127, 129, 130, 147, 150, 151, 153-5, 167, 171-3, 181, 183, 188, 198, 199
Reichert, Julie 61
Ridgway, Gregory 128, 185
Ridgway, Judith 29, 108, 110, 113, 116, 128, 130, 131, 148, 173, 176, 184, 197, 199, 200
Ridgway, Mary 16, 84, 148, 185
Ridgway, Matthew 22-4, 29, 184, 186
Ridgway, Thomas 16, 84, 169, 185, 199
Roberson, Dave 134
Roberts, Debbie 19
Rochelle, Terry 17
Rois, Carrie 9, 87, 190, 194, 204
Ross, Jeff 116, 117
Rudy, Nancy 17
Rule, Ann 175
Rule, Linda 9, 189, 203

Satterberg, Dan 132
Savage, Anthony 128, 132, 134, 136-9, 141, 144, 145 153, 154, 200

Schweiss, Bob 118
Seattle Post-Intelligencer 47, 72, 73
Seattle Times 69, 110
Shaw, Michele 134, 143
Sherrill, Shirley 9, 47, 157, 160, 189, 194, 203
Smith, Alma 9, 35, 105, 190, 193, 203
Smith, Carlton 119
Smith, Cindy 9, 68, 162, 192, 197, 205
Smith, Joseph A. 72
Spellman, Gov. John 72
Spillman, Jack 167
Stevens, Bob 113
Stevens, William Jay II 112, 113, 197
Stone, Mary Ellen 79
Stuart, Valerie 17
Summers, Shawnda 9, 45, 189, 191, 203

Taylor, Kathy 97
Theno, Roxanne 187, 193
Thomas, Vern 80, 182
Thompson, Tina 9, 64, 191, 193, 204

Urquhart, John 99, 131, 136

Ware, Kelly 9, 85, 191, 204
Weaver, Curtis 56, 105
West, Mary 9, 151
White, Dawn 64, 65
Williams, Delores 9, 190, 192, 204
Williams, Dennis Curtis 70
Wims, Cheryl 9, 89, 190, 192, 204
Winslow, Marcia 18, 23, 24, 27, 28, 75, 186
Winston, Mertie 159, 160
Winston, Tracy Ann 9
Women's Coalition to Stop the Green River Murders 78-80, 195
Woods, Robert 55

Yates, Lisa 9, 92, 192, 205
Yellowrobe, Patricia 9, 115, 119, 120, 128, 199, 205
York, Debra 101
Young, Rev. James 51

Acknowledgements

This book draws from and builds on the work of many current and former reporters, editors and photographers of the King County Journal:

Maxwell Balmain	Christopher Jarvis
Jim Bates	Pat Jenkins
Jeff Bond	Robert Jones
Steve Botkin	John Kaiser
Matt Brashears	Gary Kissel
Mike Brennan	Doug Margeson
Wini Carter	Nita Martin
Barbara Clements	Jim McNett
Brenda Day	Mark Morris
Tony Dondero	Cheryl Murfin
Marcus R. Donner	David Nelson
Scott Eklund	Nathalie Overland
Keith Ervin	Dan Partridge
Jeff Franko	Ed Penhale
Dean Forbes	Nick Perry
Robert Frank	Lyle Price
Chris Genna	Ralph Radford
Wendy Giroux	Rick Schweinhart
Deeann Glamser	Don Smith
Patrick Hagerty	Cathy Stone
Peter Haley	Mary Swift
Jim Hallas	Elaine Thompson
Duane Hamamura	Mike Ullmann
Diana Hefley	Christopher Villiers
Jan Hinman	Linda Woo

Special thanks to those who helped edit the final draft: John Huether, Rick Manugian, Tom Moore, Barbara Morgan, Christina M. Okeson, Joanne Plank and Craig Reese.

Additional copies

The King County Journal offers the first book to tell the complete, inside story of "Gary Ridgway: The Green River Killer," by the reporters who covered the case from the beginning.

More than 50 exclusive photos.

Order direct from the newspaper and save 25%.

Your name _____

Street address _____

City _____ State _____ ZIP _____

Number of copies x $12.95, minus 25% discount $9.70

shipping and handling	$1.33
8.8% sales tax	$0.97
total cost per book	$12.00
x number of books	_____
grand total	_____

Payment

___ Check enclosed

___ Bill my credit card __ Visa __ Mastercard __ Discover

Credit card number _____ Expires ___/____

Signature _____

Mail your payment and this form to:
Green River Killer book
King County Journal
1705 132nd Ave NE
Bellevue WA 98005